Social Pedagogy in Physical Education

This is the first book to examine social pedagogy within the context of physical education, enabling more inclusive, and meaningful educational experiences for all students. It introduces the key concepts of social pedagogy and outlines practical strategies for implementing social pedagogy in physical education.

Written by a team of leading international scholars and practitioners, this book assesses the research base for social pedagogy and explores how social pedagogy can be embedded in the physical education curriculum, in teaching and in assessment. Every chapter includes vignettes from both school and after-school contexts and features a practitioner voice, from a teacher or a community member. This book also looks at social pedagogy in the context of key themes across physical education, from digital assessment methods and systems thinking, to models-based approaches and physical education teacher education. As the chapters of this book unfold, the reader gets to know how to apply social pedagogy as a framework for physical education, choose strategies to enable human-centred practice, and use assessment to align the curriculum with social pedagogy principles.

This book makes a major contribution to our understanding of teaching and learning within physical education as processes of interacting for a good life though communication, connection, contribution, and creation. Concise, practical, and full of real-world examples, this is essential reading for any student, pre-service and in-service physical education teacher, or coach working with children or young people across various educational levels and country contexts.

Aspasia Dania is Assistant Professor in Physical Education Teacher Education in the School of Physical Education and Sport Science, at the National and Kapodistrian University of Athens, Greece. She teaches physical education and sport pedagogy and leads the Social Pedagogy Professional Association Special Interest Group on Social Pedagogy, Sports and Physical Education. She is also Chair-Elect of the Teaching Games for Understanding Special Interest Group. Her research interests focus on teacher education and professional development, game-based education, qualitative research methods, and curriculum planning, all focusing on social justice.

Cláudio Farias is Assistant Professor in the Faculty of Sport at the University of Porto, Portugal (FADEUP) and a research member in the Centre of Research, Education, Innovation, and Intervention in Sport (CIFI2D). He lectures on the doctoral programme, the master (hons) of physical education and sports training, and the bachelor (hons) programme in sport sciences. He has conducted research in sport pedagogy and sport coaching (physical education, teacher education, coach education) with a principal focus on student-centred, models-based practice.

Routledge Focus on Sport Pedagogy
Series editor
Ash Casey, Loughborough University, UK

The field of sport pedagogy (physical education and coaching) is united by the desire to improve the experiences of young people and adult participants. The *Routledge Focus on Sport Pedagogy* series presents small books on big topics in an effort to eradicate the boundaries that currently exist between young people, adult learners, coaches, teachers and academics, in schools, clubs and universities. Theoretically grounded but with a strong emphasis on practice, the series aims to open up important and useful new perspectives on teaching, coaching and learning in sport and physical education.

Learner-Oriented Teaching and Assessment in Youth Sport
Edited by Cláudio Farias and Isabel Mesquita

Physical Education Pedagogies for Health
Edited by Lorraine Cale and Jo Harris

Flipped Learning in Physical Education
Opportunities and Applications
Ove Østerlie, Chad Killian and Julia Sargent

Teaching Disabled Children in Physical Education
(Dis)connections between Research and Practice
Anthony J. Maher and Justin A. Haegele

Applying Models-based Practice in Physical Education
Ashley Casey and David Kirk

Social Pedagogy in Physical Education
Human-Centred Practice
Edited by Aspasia Dania and Cláudio Farias

For more information about this series, please visit: https://www.routledge.com/Routledge-Focus-on-Sport-Pedagogy/book-series/RFSPED

Social Pedagogy in Physical Education
Human-Centred Practice

**Edited by
Aspasia Dania and
Cláudio Farias**

LONDON AND NEW YORK

First published 2025
by Routledge
4 Park Square, Milton Park, Abingdon, Oxon OX14 4RN

and by Routledge
605 Third Avenue, New York, NY 10158

Routledge is an imprint of the Taylor & Francis Group, an informa business

© 2025 selection and editorial matter, Aspasia Dania and Cláudio Farias; individual chapters, the contributors

The right of Aspasia Dania and Cláudio Farias to be identified as the authors of the editorial material, and of the authors for their individual chapters, has been asserted in accordance with sections 77 and 78 of the Copyright, Designs and Patents Act 1988.

All rights reserved. No part of this book may be reprinted or reproduced or utilised in any form or by any electronic, mechanical, or other means, now known or hereafter invented, including photocopying and recording, or in any information storage or retrieval system, without permission in writing from the publishers.

Trademark notice: Product or corporate names may be trademarks or registered trademarks, and are used only for identification and explanation without intent to infringe.

British Library Cataloguing-in-Publication Data
A catalogue record for this book is available from the British Library

ISBN: 978-1-032-53332-2 (hbk)
ISBN: 978-1-032-53335-3 (pbk)
ISBN: 978-1-003-41153-6 (ebk)

DOI: 10.4324/9781003411536

Typeset in Times New Roman
by codeMantra

Contents

List of figures   xi
List of tables   xiii
List of boxes   xv
List of contributors   xvii

Introduction: Why Social Pedagogy in Physical Education?   1
ASPASIA DANIA

PART I
Social Pedagogy as a Framework for Physical Education   5

1 What Is Social Pedagogy: Connections between Theory and Practice   7
ASPASIA DANIA

2 Principles of Social Pedagogy and the Physical Education Curriculum   19
ASPASIA DANIA

PART II
Strategies for Supporting Practitioners to Use Social Pedagogy in Physical Education   31

3 A Multidisciplinary Approach to Social Pedagogy: A Pedagogical Case   33
CLÁUDIO FARIAS

4 The Syn-Epistemic Wholeness of Physical
  Education Practice 50
  ZACK BEDDOES AND EMILY JONES

5 Strategies for Enacting Social Pedagogy in Physical Education 61
  ALAN OVENS AND HANNAH STOW

PART III
The Structure of Social Pedagogy Programs as Physical Education Practice 75

6 Nurturing Activist Teachers in Physical Education
  Teacher Education 77
  CARLA NASCIMENTO LUGUETTI AND MATS HORDVIK

7 Social Pedagogy and Model-Based Approaches in
  Physical Education 89
  KANAE HANEISHI, TSE SHENG TENG, BRUCE NKALA,
  KOREY BOYD, LINDA GRIFFIN AND MAURO ANDRE

8 Social Pedagogy and Social Justice Promotion in and
  through Physical Education 104
  FERNANDO SANTOS, TARKINGTON NEWMAN, MARÍA
  FERNÁNDEZ-VILLARINO AND JILL KOCHANEK

PART IV
Assessment in and of Physical Education Programs Developed According to Social Pedagogy 119

9 Social Pedagogy and Assessment in Physical
  Education: Incorporating Students within Assessment
  Approaches 121
  SHREHAN LYNCH AND JENNIFER NORLEY

10 **Digitally Supported Assessment in Physical Education
with a Social Pedagogy Perspective** 134
ALLYSON CARVALHO DE ARAÚJO, ALISON PEREIRA
BATISTA AND MÁRCIO ROMEU RIBAS DE OLIVEIRA

**PART V
A Summary of Social Pedagogy in Physical Education** 145

11 **Insights on Social Pedagogy as Human-Centred
Physical Education Practice** 147
ASPASIA DANIA

Index 149

Figures

2.1	The Diamond Model	22
2.2	The Common Third in Physical Education	23
2.3	Change as a relational endeavour in social pedagogy	25
3.1	The social pedagogical case	39
6.1	The key PETE practices in nurturing activist teachers in becoming an activist teacher	79
7.1	Simplified flow of games based approaches	94
8.1	Social justice life skill programming continuum	107
9.1	The interrelated complexity of pedagogy	123
10.1	Organisation of the teaching unit (Authors' © 2023)	139

Tables

1.1	Concepts of Social Pedagogy (CSP) and their explanations	10
1.2	From deficit-based language towards asset-based feedback in Physical Education	13
2.1	Social pedagogy tools for Physical Education practice	26
3.1	Interconnection between social pedagogy principles and multidisciplinary contributions	38
5.1	The Student Course Committee strategy	64
5.2	Negotiating an individual learning and assessment plan with a student	65
5.3	Example of a culturally responsive teaching strategy	68
5.4	Incorporating collaborative games and activities as a social pedagogy strategy	69
5.5	The three-phase process of triadic assessment	71
7.1	Alignment to address JEDI issues by using a social pedagogy framework	94
7.2	Indicative example of lesson flow	95
9.1	Assessment point in the 'Me in Physical Education' approach	124
9.2	Example of a worksheet given to students used in athletics and dance (edited for book)	130
10.1	The prosumer concept and its relation to concepts of social pedagogy	137
10.2	Pedagogical moments of the teaching unit	141

Boxes

2.1	The Diamond Model	21
2.2	The Common Third	23
6.1	Becoming conscious about and acting against oppressive social injustices	81
6.2	Co-creating inclusive learning experiences	82
6.3	Encouraging reflection about positionality and privilege	83
6.4	Engaging in professional learning to continuously become activist teachers	84
6.5	Modelling to be and become an activist teacher	85
8.1	Operationalising social justice life skills	105
8.2	Illustrative case studies	106
8.3	Operationalisation	108
8.4	Operationalisation	108
8.5	Operationalisation	110
8.6	Key definitions	111
8.7	Progression for Physical Education teachers	113
8.8	Progression for parents	113
8.9	Progression for PETE facilitators	113

Contributors

Mauro Andre is Assistant Professor at the Physical and Health Education Teacher Education Program at Western Michigan University, USA.

Zack Beddoes is Assistant Professor in Physical Education Teacher Education, at the Brigham Young University in Provo, Utah, USA.

Korey Boyd is Assistant Professor at the School of Physical Education, Performance, and Sport Leadership at Springfield College, Massachusetts, USA.

Allyson Carvalho de Araújo is Associate Professor in the Department of Physical Education at the Federal University of Rio Grande do Norte, Brazil.

María Fernández-Villarino is Associate Professor in the Faculty of Educational Sciences and Sport at the University of Vigo, Spain.

Linda Griffin is Professor of Sport Pedagogy in the College of Education at the University of Massachusetts, Amherst, USA.

Kanae Haneishi is Associate Professor of Exercise and Sport Science at Western Colorado University, USA.

Emily Jones is Professor of Physical Education Teacher Education in the School of Kinesiology and Recreation at Illinois State University, USA.

Jill Kochanek is Assistant Professor and Athletic Leadership Master's Program Director at Springfield College, Massachusetts, USA.

Shrehan Lynch is Senior Lecturer and Course Leader for the Sport Foundation Degree at the University of East London, UK.

Mats Hordvik is Associate Professor in Physical Education Teacher Education at the Norwegian School of Sport Sciences, Norway.

Carla Nascimento Luguetti is Lecturer in Health and Physical Education at the Faculty of Education, University of Melbourne.

Tarkington Newman is Associate Professor at the College of Social Work, at the University of Kentucky, USA.

Bruce Nkala is Athletic Director at Sandy Spring Friends School, Maryland, USA.

Jennifer Norley is a Physical Education Teacher with a master's degree from King's College, London, UK.

Alan Ovens is Associate Professor and Discipline Leader of Sport, Health, and Physical Education at the University of Auckland, New Zealand.

Alison Pereira Batista holds a master and doctoral degree in Education from the Federal University of Rio Grande do Norte, Brazil.

Márcio Romeu Ribas de Oliveira is Associate Professor in the Department of Physical Education at the Federal University of Rio Grande do Norte, Brazil.

Fernando Santos is Associate Professor at Polytechnic Institute of Porto, Higher School of Education in Portugal.

Tse Sheng Teng is a Physical Education Master Teacher with the Physical Education and Sports Teacher Academy (PESTA).

Hannah Stow is a Health and Physical Education teacher, graduate from the University of Auckland, New Zealand.

Introduction
Why Social Pedagogy in Physical Education?

Aspasia Dania

From the outset, we want to stress that this is more than another book on pedagogy or pedagogical practice. Instead, it embraces our perspective for creating a nurturing learning and growth environment where our students can flourish and unfold their full potential through Physical Education. In our view, social pedagogy has the potential to significantly re-orientate school Physical Education to create a more inclusive, meaningful, and socially just educational experience for young people. The idea that social pedagogy can transform Physical Education programmes sets this book apart from others.

Our first goal with this book is to propose social pedagogy as a holistic approach for nurturing young people through shared Physical Education experiences, which acknowledges them as intrinsically rich and resourceful. How this is achieved and the methods, strategies, or affordances required to achieve this goal will vary within and between different countries. In some countries, social pedagogy is an academic discipline that supports social education and social work, while in other countries, social pedagogy and social work have either merged into one profession or social pedagogy is a profession in its own right. Despite this variation, our goal is to actively promote social pedagogy as a new paradigm in school Physical Education and see movement contexts and activities as core spaces for holistic learning.

Our second goal is to encourage practitioners to think of social pedagogy as the means through which students' ability for freedom, transformation, and change can be achieved. For this purpose, in all chapters of the book, we examine the 'pedagogy – Physical Education' connection in response to interactions, ideas, needs, things, spaces, and relationships occurring through various levels (e.g., personal, family, school, community) and instructional systems of practice (e.g., actors, artefacts, activities, tasks). In this sense, we envision this goal as being about seeing the outcomes of Physical Education going beyond the 'physical' to include social, emotional, spiritual, and cultural growth.

For this reason, we use the terms 'physical education' and 'social pedagogy' (with lowercase initial letters) to refer to the relationality and co-construction of the educational process and 'Physical Education' (with uppercase initial letters) to refer to the school subject per se. We avoid using 'PE' as a stylistic abbreviation since we believe that it can bring the opposite effects to our effort, especially regarding the negative experiences that many people may have from their participation in narrow education practices that reinforce schooling and compartmentalised learning through Physical Education (e.g., blueprint instructional models that guide the use of specific practices, short blocks of unrelated physical activities, etc.). We also avoid using the term 'Social Pedagogy' (with higher case initial letters) since, on the one hand, we claim for many 'Social Pedagogies' and on the other hand, we seek to introduce pedagogy as philosophy-in-use and not as a new discipline in the field of educational sciences.

The content presented in this book is divided into five main sections. Part I, 'Social Pedagogy as a Framework for Physical Education', introduces the philosophy and principles of social pedagogy and key concepts concerning how social pedagogy is understood and needs to be delivered in Physical Education according to the specificities of different sociocultural contexts. Part II, 'Strategies for Supporting Practitioners to Use Social Pedagogy in Physical Education', explores the pedagogical and instructional strategies that need to be employed by practitioners who wish to apply social pedagogy in and through Physical Education. Part III, 'The Structure of Social Pedagogy Programs as Physical Education Practice', presents concrete examples for developing and implementing social pedagogy programmes across various contexts (e.g., in and out of school) and education levels (e.g., primary, secondary). Part IV, 'Assessment in and of Physical Education Programs Developed according to Social Pedagogy', presents a set of recommendations for promoting assessment within Physical Education programmes under a social pedagogy perspective. Finally, Part V, 'A Summary of Social Pedagogy in Physical Education', answers the question *What is social pedagogy in Physical Education?* by synthesising key points addressed in all the book chapters.

Each part allows room for multiple international understandings by identifying the scope and nature of social pedagogy in Physical Education through three ideological models: the adaptive model (e.g., social integration by treatment), the mobilising model (e.g., emancipation by joint action), and the democratic model (e.g., social cohesion through active citizenship). This makes the contribution of this book both timely and relevant considering (a) the fast-paced changes in education as a response to societies' digitally infused acceleration, (b) the need to (re)claim the status of Physical Education as an important locus for education, and (c) the joint effort of co-authors/experts who use this book as an international opportunity for the enactment of social pedagogy as praxis within Physical Education.

All contributors in the book were asked to engage with social pedagogy as a topic that they believed could contribute new dimensions to the study of educational theory and practice in Physical Education. Their valuable and expert contribution created a resource informed by up-to-date knowledge from various fields of professional experience that can help practitioners plan, implement, and assess Physical Education lessons from a social pedagogy perspective. We believe that this book will stimulate interest in teacher and practitioner contexts and enable future collaborative and translational research projects in professional learning and development communities.

As physical educators working in various countries and university contexts worldwide, we engage critically with social pedagogy and its connection to curriculum, instruction, and assessment in Physical Education. Even though for all of us, social pedagogy is a new field of enquiry, we are eager to present our shared perspective on how social pedagogy can be introduced as a values-led approach to relationship-centred practice in Physical Education. We feel that such an effort is rather important given that social pedagogy aims at promoting wellbeing, learning, and social inclusion concerning more prominent social issues and not only at an individual or group level.

Part I
Social Pedagogy as a Framework for Physical Education

1 What Is Social Pedagogy

Connections between Theory and Practice

Aspasia Dania

Learning Objectives

At the end of this chapter, you will be able to:

- Name various perspectives of social pedagogy theory and practice.
- Provide a rationale for social pedagogy in Physical Education.
- Explain the connections between social pedagogy theory and Physical Education practice.

VIGNETTE

I am a Physical Education teacher working in primary education for the last ten years. I am currently a doctoral candidate in Physical Education teacher education, and as part of my research, I am studying different pedagogical approaches. When I first read about social pedagogy, I was not sure about what was meant by 'social' and how 'pedagogy' could relate to that meaning. I initially assumed that social pedagogy refers to a teaching approach or strategy that uses social science content for educational purposes. I found this view relatively narrow, so I kept exploring how the notion of social pedagogy could fit into Physical Education. My readings enabled me to approach 'pedagogy' in its broader role (i.e., as holistic development and support of young people) and the 'social' as a denominator of education. I understood that social pedagogy refers to the work done by teachers (e.g., educational work, care) on behalf of society to help young people act with reason, respect, and equity in their lives. I thought that from a social pedagogy perspective, Physical Education teachers could be professionals who may help children and youth be open to good things in their lives and generate a broader sense of achievement at an individual, group, community, and social level. I believe that if we adopted social pedagogy in Physical Education, we would focus more on what it means to be human and what is the image of the young person for whom

DOI: 10.4324/9781003411536-3

we envisage education in interaction with others and with life (I think in German literature, this process is referred to as Bildung). I found this perspective rather valuable for creating conditions of belonging and connectedness within my classes, and that is why I decided to deepen my understanding of social pedagogy and its relation to the work of physical educators.

Introduction

Social pedagogy is a values-led approach to supporting the development of youth through practices that are relationship-centred. Its fundamental principle is that it builds on learners' previous experiences to generate learning, care, health, and wellbeing, all established and integrated in the relationships that they (can) have with others. By acknowledging that every learner deserves to be treated with human dignity, social pedagogues advocate for education as the creation of a strong sense of community. Thus, social pedagogy is both pedagogy – in the form of upbringing, support, and care – and education, with education occurring both in formal (i.e., schools) and informal contexts (communities, families, care centres, etc.). A distinguishing feature is that social pedagogues view themselves as inhabiting the same life space as their learners and working with them within activities that integrate body, mind, emotions, and spirit. The goal is to enhance learners' self-esteem and sense of possibility to navigate effectively within their lives' flaws, ambiguities, and discrepancies.

Social pedagogy can generate insights that are well-adjusted to the complexity of modern educational realities. Therefore, this chapter proposes elements for reflection and analysis that could help readers understand social pedagogy and its relation to educational praxis (i.e., theory and practice). The idea is to provide a framework for integrating social pedagogy within Physical Education and explore its potential contribution to improving school practice in a spirit of hope and human solidarity. To achieve this aim, the chapter is divided into three sections. The first section provides a rationale for working with social pedagogy in Physical Education. In the second section, the focus is shed on the connection between social pedagogy theory and Physical Education practice. The third section (advice from the field of Physical Education) highlights the need to reconceptualise the socio-pedagogical relation and integrate social pedagogy as a pedagogy of care and support in Physical Education.

Rationale for Social Pedagogy in Physical Education

We use social pedagogy theory as the focus of this book since we intend to adopt a broader view of Physical Education as a field of social progress and reform. We believe social pedagogy can add value to Physical Education since it conceptualises learning as a relational process. For social pedagogy, education and empowerment never end. That is what the teacher in the vignette suggests 'education in its broader sense' and the 'social as a denominator of education'. Thus, Physical Education teachers can use social pedagogy principles to support young learners in learning and growing through the relationships they develop with others or the activities they adopt as contexts of relational learning. The social pedagogue does not use pre-established or 'one-size-fits-all' standards to generate learning outcomes. Instead, they use methods and techniques within a shared life space with learners and engage with them in various activities to give rise to desired effects (e.g., interest, motivation, devotion, critical thinking). Using this logic, Physical Education teachers will not seek to give immediate solutions/guidelines to problems that children and youth may face (e.g., lack of physical activity, inequality, etc.). However, it is clear that these are the ultimate objectives in the long run. Instead, they will primarily seek care, assistance, empowerment, and supervision to mobilise students as learners to adopt a particular way of thinking or acting instead of another. In this sense, socially informed Physical Education pedagogy can be extended within and outside the school context. It seeks to support young learners in making their own decisions, relationally, about whatever affects them. As suggested by the teacher in the vignette at the beginning of this chapter, this process is referred to as *Bildung*.

Social pedagogy is interpreted differently in each country (i.e., context), depending on the national, cultural, ethnic, or local context (e.g., beliefs, behaviour patterns, values, etc.). Thus, we seek to identify as many 'social pedagogies' as possible, depending on the cultural, disciplinary, and contextual dimensions. Since we acknowledge the importance of social pedagogy variations, the scope of this book is to embrace cross-cultural or trans-disciplinary understandings of social pedagogy as an opportunity to shed light on how social issues can be developed into pedagogical questions within Physical Education. To provide insight into our thinking, we present a hypothetical discussion between a social pedagogy professor (pseudonym Judy Palmer) and a Physical Education teacher (pseudonym Andrew Weber) to highlight how key dimensions and features of social pedagogy could be integrated as theory and practice in Physical Education. Within the discussion, fundamental *Concepts of Social Pedagogy* (*CSP*) are highlighted and further explained in Table 1.1.

These concepts are further explored throughout the book chapters to shape the discussion around the value of socially informed Physical Education practice.

Time for Dialogue: How Do You Combine Social Pedagogy Theory and Physical Education Practice?

ANDREW WEBER (AW):   Professor Judy Palmer, I would like to welcome and thank you for accepting my invitation to discuss social pedagogy as Physical Education practice.

JUDY PALMER (JP): Thank you Mr Weber. I think it is always beneficial to dialogue about the many ways that we can combine theory, policy, and practice in education.

AW: "…Indeed. That is why, through the years, we have been trying to achieve a balance between what we conceive of as individual emancipation and social integration in Physical Education. For this reason, we have been eager to find ways of dealing with social exclusion and improve the welfare of children and youth. We have worked to develop program alternatives to elite sport and policies that improve individual and social well-being. Our focus has been the betterment of our students' everyday lives. Thus, we believe that social pedagogy can play a crucial role in human development, social support, and care, especially for those vulnerable in Physical Education…"

JP: "…Yes, I can see what you mean. Historically, social pedagogy has focused on problems such as poverty, social exclusion, and many others by aiming to improve the welfare of disadvantaged or vulnerable people. For social pedagogy, group life and activities that unite people play an important role in human development (*CSP: Common Third*). Therefore, shared activities help people understand themselves as social beings and extend their perception of societal membership. The goal is to recognise the optimal conditions for social integration within a given society."

Table 1.1 Concepts of Social Pedagogy (CSP) and their explanations*

CSP	Explanation
The Common Third	Activities that strengthen relationships between the teacher and the learners
	Shared activities that become an experience of togetherness which distracts power hierarchies
Head – Heart – Hands	**Head** stands for the knowledge (theory & rationality) that the pedagogues need to have to support learners effectively
	Heart stands for the pedagogues' unconditional acceptance and engagement with learners at an emotional level with passion, compassion, and genuine beliefs
	Hands stand for the pedagogues' acting-as-knowledge and information about the learners and acting-as-understanding of what works or not

(*Continued*)

Table 1.1 (Continued)

CSP	Explanation
Participation & Preparing for Participation	People need to prepare for Participation by having... ...access to those in power ...access to information ...real choice between different options ...support from a trusted person ...an appeal or complaint process **Participation means being able to...** ...listen actively ...meet and reflect on assumptions ...share and safeguard information ...prepare for interacting with others ...make their decisions ...reflect on decisions for change
The Diamond Model (Well-Being, Happiness, Empowerment)	**Well-Being and Happiness mean...** • Compassion • Responsibility • Collaborations • Curiosity • Creativity and Flourishing **Empowerment means...** • Person-Centred support • Bringing our own selves to class • Appreciation & feedback • Taking Risks & Learning • Celebrating • Trusting & Sharing information
Creativity	**Creativity means...** Using imagination as co-production Pursuing purpose and avoiding linear approaches to problem solving Originality as authentic solutions Judging value as worth
The three Ps (Professional, Personal, Private)	**The three Ps of social pedagogy...** Professional – engagement with knowledge, research, practice, evidence- theory for a specific purpose Personal – Reciprocity as a strength-based approach to resilience promotion and relationship building Private – All that is shared is done with the purpose to benefit the individual

* Throughout the book's chapters, Concepts of Social Pedagogy are highlighted as CSP, and an explanation of their meaning is given by referring to Table 1.1.

AW: "...For me, growth as emancipation is important. Children and youth possess certain personal qualities. Our intention as Physical Education teachers is to accompany them in their everyday efforts or struggles to accumulate resources that allow them to live in a dignified manner. They live their lives; they experience and understand them with their minds, bodies, and spirits (*CSP: Head-Heart-Hands*). What we can do is help them develop strategies for critically selecting their unified ways of being or living in the world. We must give our best to expand their capabilities for action and help them understand that action means commitment to a goal ..."

JP: "...You raise an important issue here. With social pedagogy, we perceive that children and youth are rich in potential and, most of all, connected to adults and other children. We are not looking at what they are lacking. We are eager to find out how young learners can be encouraged to become aware of their present situation to expand their capabilities for action by valuing themselves. Either within shared activities of teaching and learning together (*CSP: Participation*), or within activities that encourage personal, social, and moral education (*CSP: Preparing for Participation*), social pedagogy sets the basis for establishing conditions for fulfilment and agency..."

AW: "...That is, I guess, the reason why we must be very humble in goal-setting when we work with individuals in social pedagogy. They need to see themselves as joint participants in bringing change to their lives. Especially with children and youth, we need to prioritise activities that help them disengage from dominant individual-centred *deficit traps*. We also need to remember that if youth face severe life circumstances – like poverty, for example – they might not participate in our programs, even those that target their developmental needs...".

JP: "...That is exactly what I meant. The *deficit or therapeutic* perspective assumes that young people from disadvantaged areas or situations need support since they are uniformly deficient (Coakley, 2016). This is a narrow perspective since it distracts attention from the social system circumstances that may make young

Table 1.2 From deficit-based language towards asset-based feedback in Physical Education

	Deficit Feedback		Asset-Based Feedback
Instead of saying....	...You are not doing enough exercise yet...	Say....	...Looks like you are getting the hang of exercise...
	...I know you need more time to practice with your basketball shooting skills, you will get better with practice...		...Your basketball shooting skills are so much better because you took time to practice more systematically...
	...If you don't have a quiet space at home to practice, you can come to school earlier. The gym is open every morning before school time...		...A quiet environment is something that you said will be good for you. You can come to the gym in the morning before school, I go there earlier as well...
	...We all learn from failure. Just keep trying to do your best...		...You never give up when you are playing that video game you like. Use this perseverance to keep trying in the Physical Education class...

people vulnerable (e.g., poverty and inequalities) (Haudenhuyse et al., 2013). Within social pedagogy, we seek to critically understand and explain social phenomena before suggesting activities or programs. One unique characteristic of our strategy is asset-based feedback (see Table 1.2). Asset-based feedback provides information about what learners already know and can do, introduces learning pathways to help them meet the expectations, and identifies strategies they can adopt to use their strengths to meet learning needs..."

AW: "...We need to build supportive networks that may help some young people stand stronger in society. If they do not want to change, we can do nothing else but wait until they are ready to receive our help. We should not forget that we work with people, not structures, and they have their own voice to speak about or decide what they want or can do in their own circumstances...."

JP: "...Yes, social pedagogy has an ideological foundation oriented towards social justice. We can say that social pedagogy is political in that its theory interrogates both how society informs pedagogy and how various pedagogies – either those employed in addressing marginalised groups or more general ones – inform society. Social pedagogy does not seek to prescribe or regulate behaviours. Instead, it seeks to guide and help people develop critical awareness and adaptability. That is why we believe very much in dialogue and engagement with others. We need our learners to be able to act in a respectful, equitable and satisfactory level when it comes to real-life problems..."

AW: "...I agree. I think we need to escape the political trap when we think about social pedagogy. Pedagogy cannot provide quick-time solutions to structural problems or injustices in society. This is neither its goal nor its mission..."

JP: "...Exactly. If politics is inspiration, then pedagogy is expiration. When we talk about *children in need, what we see at an educational policy level is a need to create policies* and interventions for the welfare of these children. I think that social pedagogy moves the focus from the scope of *NEED* to the act and experience of *FREEDOM* in everyday life (*CSP: The Diamond Model*). For social pedagogy, a *child in need* has the capability for agency and freedom. Therefore, we can enable children to get out of any precarious situation by engaging with them in everyday activities based on their value as human beings ..."

AW: "...We certainly build on the idea of transdisciplinarity when we refer to social pedagogy..."

JP: "...Yes, at a professional level, social pedagogy has strong connections with professions that share the *social* as a sphere of action, such as social work, pedagogy, and social education. However, since the *social* subsumes cultural, political, environmental, and digital fields of action, it is better to refer to social pedagogies (rather than social pedagogy) when referring to professions that produce norms, principles, and social work for different societies. What remains at the focus of all social pedagogies is not what kind of norms are produced, but instead where and for whom these norms are headed for..."

AW: "...I guess you mean that understanding what *social* means has changed over the years. So, speaking of standardised social pedagogical norms in Physical Education would make no sense. The practices and strategies used by Physical Education teachers, social pedagogues, youth, and community workers are all dependent on the ideologies enacted within the disciplinary traditions of each socio-cultural and political-economic context. For example, present-day school Physical Education is acknowledged as an educational field overseeing physical activities such as games, sport, leisure, and recreation. In all these physical activities, sportive attitudes (e.g., competition, performance at all costs, etc.) are present..."

JP: "...Since Physical Education has a prominent presence in many fields of the social space (e.g., schools, playgrounds, recreation, etc.), such attitudes are transferred to society (*CSP: Creativity*). Thus, if we do not care about the 'how, what and for whom' in Physical Education, we may misrepresent or reproduce unfairness and inequity. We do not work for people; we co-create with them ..."

AW: "...What I perceive is that we need a generous interaction between different professional fields – maybe in the form of open dialogue – to understand what good living is for each individual and each different community or society and how Physical Education pedagogy attributes itself to the complexity of social reality..."

JP: "...At an epistemological level, social pedagogy is both a science and an art since it is being oriented in, by and towards practice. What differentiates social pedagogy from other pedagogies is the concept of the learner and his/her relationship with the world. Relationships are essential to socio-pedagogical actions (e.g., pedagogy or relationships, relationships that consciously bring care, etc.). Thus, the social pedagogue seeks theoretical and practical support to construct rules of action for individuals, extending relationships that can stimulate and assist their growth and development (*CSP: The Three Ps*). We should note that *what works well* mentalities or evidence-based norms are not prioritised. Instead, the dignity of each individual and the commitment to a good life are the focal points..."

AW: "...What matters in our programs when we use social pedagogy principles is their quality in terms of the closeness and caring relationships developed with our learners. I do not mean that we are not interested in professional codes of conduct or the production of scientific evidence or learning objectives. We evaluate our interventions' results and ensure their implementation fidelity. However, we do not put evaluation first to demonstrate evidence to external observers about fulfilling expected learning outcomes. We respect the rights of our students and try to prioritise the social act itself, avoiding the delivery of standardised services or one-size-fits-all welfare measures. Consolidation, accompaniment, caring, and warmth are our commitment…"

JP: "…. I like the notion of care, and I agree with Noddings' (2002) definition of caring relations. For Noddings (2002, p. 19) A and B are in a caring encounter if and only if:

- **A cares for B**, meaning that A's consciousness is characterised by attention and motivational displacement
- **A performs** some 'I' act, and
- **B recognises** that A cares for B.

For Physical Education, this would mean that teaching is experienced as a calling drawn out of the self and seeking to see 'the other's reality as a possibility for my own' (Noddings, 1984/2003, p. 14).

Key Points

- Social pedagogy is a values-led approach to supporting the development of children and young people, through relationship-centred practices.
- Social pedagogy is both pedagogy and education, with education happening in and out of schools.
- In social pedagogy, emphasis is put on practices that integrate body, mind, emotions, and spirit.

Advice from the Field

Aspasia Dania (Greece, Physical Education Teacher Education, Author)

In many Physical Education programmes worldwide, the development of young people is envisaged mostly as an individual process that does not consider the need for collective action, or social change at a community level. With reference to the so-called 'heartfelt narratives' (Hartmann & Kwauk, 2011), Physical Education units or courses are designed with a goal to address young people's deficits and train their skills to overcome barriers. In our everyday Physical Education discourse, self-esteem, decision-making, leadership, gender attitudes, knowledge about health and many others have become *everyday words*. My impression is that we adopt these words rather naively when we assume that if we 'boost' for example decision making or self-esteem via physical activity and exercise, we will foster positive youth outcomes. I am afraid that if we remain uncritical towards this type of thinking we may harm young people and their future self-image. What if they don't make it to achieve medium to high levels of physical activity daily? Will that be considered a personal failure? What it means for girls in the long term to be more inactive than boys? We need to be careful when we make assumptions about the deficits that youth may have or face. As teachers, mentors, or facilitators of young people we need to reflect on how we could become better for supporting them. Some points we could reflect on as part of our daily practice include:

- Do we know our learners well enough?
- Do we engage in dialogue with them to understand their needs?
- Do we seek for the best opportunities to support them?
- Do we afford ourselves time for reflecting on our relationship with our learners?
- Do we seek for support from colleagues, families, or community professionals in our effort to better understand our learners and help them achieve their full potential?

Social pedagogy gives us an opportunity to work with youth development both at an individual and at a community or institutional level. I think that this can be a great starting point for uncovering the fault assumptions of the deficit model and help youth construct new understandings, based on what they already know and are able to do.

Summary

Social pedagogy builds on people's previous experiences to generate relationship-centred learning, care, health, and well-being. At the beginning of this chapter, a Physical Education teacher admitted that when teachers understand the meaning and value of social pedagogy, they are eager afterwards to use it in their classrooms to create conditions of belonging and connectedness.

That is why in the present chapter, we embraced existing discussions on social pedagogy as an opportunity to expand its value as knowledge and practice within Physical Education. By presenting a fictional discussion between a social pedagogy expert and a Physical Education teacher, we showed how social pedagogy's use within Physical Education could improve theory and practice. Our idea of a socially informed Physical Education pedagogy builds on care, assistance, and supervision as strategies needed to mobilise young learners to expand their capabilities for action by living in the world with their body, mind, emotions, and spirit.

Reflection Questions and Activities

1 "…When I care … there is a motivational shift. My motive energy flows toward the other and perhaps, although not necessarily, toward his ends.…. I allow my motive energy to be shared…". (Noddings, 1984/2003, p. 33).

After reading Noddings' statement above, list at least three reasons about why you think it is important for a teacher to care for his/her students.

References

Coakley, J. (2016). Positive youth development through sport: Myths, beliefs, and realities. In N. Holt (Eds.), *Positive youth development through sport* (pp. 21–33). Routledge.

Hartmann, D., & Kwauk, C. (2011). Sport and development: An overview, critique, and reconstruction. *Journal of Sport and Social Issues*, *35*(3), 284–305. https://doi.org/10.1177/0193723511416986

Haudenhuyse, R., Theeboom, M., & Nols, Z. (2013). Sports-based interventions for socially vulnerable youth: Towards well-defined interventions with easy-to-follow outcomes? *International Review for the Sociology of Sport*, *48*(4), 471–484. https://doi.org/10.1177/1012690212448002

Noddings, N. (2002). *Starting at home: Caring and social policy*. University of California Press.

Noddings, N. (1984/2003). *Happiness and education*. Cambridge University Press. https://doi.org/10.1017/CBO9780511499920

Additional Resources

- Úcar, X. (2021). Constructing questions for the social professions of today: The case of social pedagogy. *International Journal of Social Pedagogy*, *10*(1), 1–13. https://doi.org/10.14324/111.444.ijsp.2021.v10.1.009
- Úcar, X, Soler-Masó, P., & Planas-Lladó, A. (2020). *Working with young people: A social pedagogy perspective from Europe and Latin America*. Oxford University Press.

2 Principles of Social Pedagogy and the Physical Education Curriculum

Aspasia Dania

Learning Objectives

At the end of this chapter, you will be able to:

- Identify basic principles of social pedagogic work in Physical Education.
- Understand social pedagogic practices and the way they can be used within the Physical Education curriculum.

VIGNETTE

Mrs Johnson is a Physical Education teacher at a high school in the UK. The lesson has already begun, and students are practising a yoga routine. When Mrs Johnson spots Mary and Nina entering the gymnasium late and talking to each other loudly, she says: "Please, girls, lower your voice when entering the classroom". This is a boundary/rule that Mrs Johnson has set for her Physical Education classroom. Mary and Nina seemed in no mood to listen to their teacher, so they continued talking to each other while walking to the side of the gymnasium. Mrs Johnson repeats: "Can you please walk silently when you arrive late at the gymnasium after the start of the lesson?" The two students choose to ignore their teacher again, so Mrs Johnson walks close to them and says:

> Mary and Nina, I would like to let you know that when you walk into the gymnasium while laughing and talking loudly, the lesson is interrupted by the noise you make. We have all worked together today to establish a peaceful atmosphere for our yoga routine, so I'd like you to help me keep it peaceful. Can you please pick up a mattress as quickly as possible so that you can join us silently in practice?

In social pedagogy, this is a confrontational learning technique.

Introduction

Social pedagogy adopts a view of education as *Bildung*,[1] aiming at human growth and initiative. Our goal when working with social pedagogy is to accompany young people in learning and acquiring resources for their lives. During this process, we may use various principles of action to help them improve their life circumstances, develop self-care routines, endure hardship, and build resilience. It is important to note that social pedagogy puts people, not structures (e.g., curriculum), at the focus. This emphasises the complexities of human nature and its unique patterns of interaction. Some of the humanistic values upon which social pedagogy is based are:

- The child or the young person is supported as a whole person who develops and interacts closely with others within a group.
- The teacher sees herself/himself inhabiting the same life space with young people, not as existing in separate hierarchical domains.
- Teachers and students come together to negotiate decisions and roles.
- The centrality of relationships is important for the facilitation of communication and listening.
- Youth's associative life is seen as an important resource for developing action.
- Parents and community members' contributions in 'bringing up' children are also acknowledged (Cameron et al., 2021).

Social pedagogy pays special attention to the preconditions of human growth and the pedagogical opportunities that can influence and promote this growth. For this purpose, the young person is encountered as an agent (and not simply as a learner), and the school is organised as a space for deliberative and democratic living (and not only as a site for curriculum engagement). At the beginning of this chapter, Mrs Johnson tries to clarify that for the two students who enter the gymnasium by being loud and disrespectful to their peers' efforts. Within this process, the role of the teacher is vital in facilitating school-community collaborations and offering a pedagogical perspective that will connect people with their moral values.

By adopting the above assumptions, the goal of this chapter is to introduce social pedagogy within Physical Education "…as a mission aimed at developing each student's commitment, openness, wonder [and] passion' of learning…" (Dall'Alba & Barnacle, 2007, p. 681). There are three factors that motivated this endeavour:

1 The first is our commitment as Physical Education teacher educators to facilitate youth to deliberately choose who/what they want to be/become in their relationships with others (e.g., teachers, peers, family).
2 The second is our mission to inform Physical Education teachers about the ways they can work with students to help them commit to change and progress in their lives.

3 The third is our need to valorise the Physical Education curriculum as a context which displaces the seer transmission of skills and knowledge and forwards pedagogy as an emergent process of co-orchestration of abilities, rights, and values.

To achieve this goal, the chapter is divided into two parts. The first part presents three principles that need to guide the teacher's work when using social pedagogy in Physical Education. Within each principle, key social pedagogy concepts are outlined. The second part presents pedagogical practices as how-to examples of working with social pedagogy within Physical Education. The idea is not to present the organisational structure of a social pedagogic classroom but instead, give an outline of the holistic and relationship-centred way that Physical Education teachers could adopt when working with social pedagogy in educational settings or youth (care) centres.

Social Pedagogy Principles in Physical Education

Principle One: Work with Children and Youth

A fundamental social pedagogy principle is that teachers *work with* rather than *work for* children and youth. From a social pedagogic perspective, young people are experts in their lives and efficient in developing action. Thus, teachers are primarily concerned with young people and who they want to become. This richness that all people have in terms of knowledge, skills and abilities is symbolised in social pedagogy by the *Diamond Model* (Eichsteller & Holthoff, 2012). With a benevolent concern for children and youth, the Physical Education teacher who chooses to work with the *Diamond Model* (Box 2.1) starts from the unfailing belief in intrinsic human value and introduces activities that (a) appreciate the thinking and doing of every student, and (b) signal the value of solidarity, kindness, and social justice. The goal is to enhance students' well-being and happiness and help them 'shine as diamonds' in school and out-of-school life (Figure 2.1). For this purpose, activities that may stimulate and/or empower learners to work with their mind, body, feelings, and spirit, as well as relational activities that aim at developing within-group connections

---

Box 2.1   The Diamond Model

Social pedagogy's *Diamond Model* (Eichsteller & Holthoff, 2012) symbolises the power of individuals and communities to flourish by co-creating experiences that foster holistic learning and empower people to take charge of their own lives. *Positive learning experiences, holistic development, relationships, and empowerment are the key components of the Diamond Model.*

Figure 2.1 The Diamond Model.

and learners' interdependence, are used. The goal is to safeguard young people's engagement and long-term commitment to life in the classroom so that behaviour management or trauma regulation activities are not required.

Principle Two: Relationships Are Mediators of Teaching and Learning

A second principle of social pedagogy is its relation-centred approach to teaching and learning. Based on this principle, *participation in classroom activities becomes the context, the medium and the content of learning.* From a social pedagogic perspective, the teacher requests students to give their best to the 'common good', to be respectful of the efforts of others, and to show empathy and care for their peers. This is rather evident in how Mrs Johnson (in the opening vignette) handles the situation during her class. To help students do their best, the teacher can use the *Common Third* (Box 2.2) as a critical concept for building strong classroom relationships to facilitate meaningful lesson participation for all students. The *Common Third* refers to using any activity/idea that can strengthen the teacher-student relationship (Figure 2.2). For example, the Physical Education teacher may choose to work with ethical behaviours within a Sport Education unit. By adopting the *Common Third*, the teacher will design and implement activities within which students will have multiple opportunities to work with positive reinforcement to peers, discussion in small groups, non-judgemental feedback, respect and responsibility for action, as ideas that are relevant to ethical classroom behaviours. The teacher's goal will be to help students establish relationships of trust, reciprocity, and authenticity within the shared space of the Sport Education unit.

Box 2.2 The Common Third

The *Common Third* refers to any kind of activity/idea that creates a commonly shared situation within which something third (e.g., playing football together, preparing the festivity event in Sport Education, etc.) brings the teacher and the students to learn and interact together. As part of this activity, small group discussions, debriefings on the relationship between right-thinking and right-doing can also be integrated, as a way of putting values alive in practice both as content and as medium of learning.

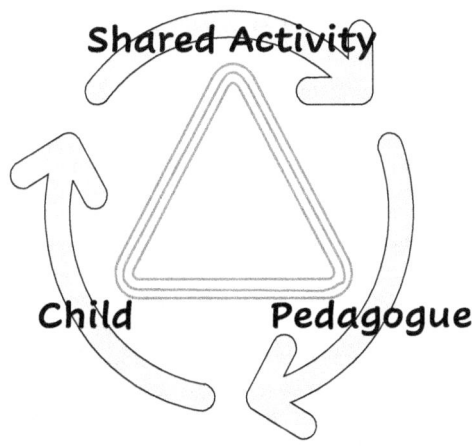

Figure 2.2 The Common Third in Physical Education.

Principle Three: Students Are Helped to Decide How They Want to Educate Themselves

A third principle of social pedagogy is that education and empowerment are attained and achieved with no end through the relationships people establish and the activities they choose to do. Social pedagogues don't educate but get students to decide and choose how to educate themselves. Within this process, students negotiate with forces and influences inherent in their physical, virtual, and socio-cultural settings and either adopt or confront them. Social pedagogy aims to accompany and facilitate youth in this effort in equitable and sustainable ways for their growth and progress. The teacher's role is to accompany students in their struggles and allow them to choose the capacities and attitudes with which they will respond. In such a perspective, the Physical Education teacher does not seek to educate students or train their skills and abilities. Instead, he/she aims to empower them to acquire the resources they need to construct their ways of (well)being and educating themselves. To do so, the teacher may employ activities and/or actions committed to participatory democracy processes. For example, the Physical Education teacher who uses modified games as part of a game-based unit needs to ensure that all students – rather than only their elected representatives – can get involved in decisions related to their game tactics or strategies. Even though there are various levels of participatory democracy practices (e.g., information, consultation, dialogue, and partnership), all need to engage students actively in decision-making processes that will positively affect their learning experiences. Activities that can support the implementation of participatory democracy practices are activities that focus on *Communication, Connection, Contribution, and Creation (4Cs)* within various parts of the lesson. Within social pedagogy, the *4Cs* are used to design activities that sensitise students to equity, diversity, and social justice issues.

Social Pedagogy Practices in Physical Education

When we adopt social pedagogy in Physical Education, we seek to change how teachers and students work together to address real-life needs and circumstances in school and out-of-school settings. *Relationships* are the medium through which teachers work with students on commonly decided goals within activities or practices with a situationally relevant *structure*. *Change* will afterwards occur as the outcome of this relational work (Figure 2.3). It is essential at this point to clarify that when we refer to relational change, we mean all those small changes that may occur through bottom-up processes (e.g., adoption of active learning strategies, shared decision-making activities, reflection and sharing of ideas, etc.). Top-down procedures for implementing norms and standards do not align with the relational nature of social pedagogy.

We cannot have social pedagogic work in Physical Education without a goal of (pedagogical) change. For example, a Physical Education classroom that does not support all students towards achieving their desired goals (e.g., to be more physically active, to enjoy playing with peers, etc.), is another place to keep students busy and happy. Similarly, we cannot discuss social pedagogic change if a change occurs outside the Physical Education classroom structure. Social pedagogy is a relational sphere, and change is inextricably linked to the person-in-the-community. Thus, even if we observe a change in attitudes towards physical activity (e.g., due to the attendance of a short seminar), if this change is not the outcome of relational work, it cannot be treated as social pedagogic.

Principles of Social Pedagogy and Physical Education Curriculum 25

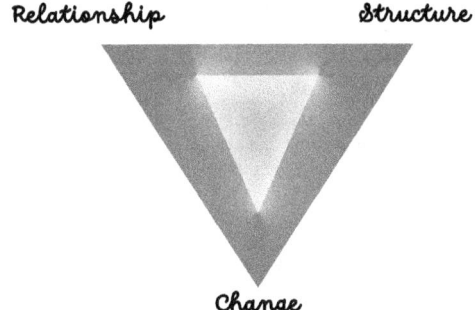

Figure 2.3 Change as a relational endeavour in social pedagogy.

In the following section (see Table 2.1), we offer examples of practices and/or tools to inspire Physical Education teachers who wish to apply social pedagogy in their classrooms. As already mentioned in Chapter 1, social pedagogy does not provide a normative synthesis of practices that could guide all physical educators' work towards the same expected learning outcomes. Social pedagogic practice is contextual. Thus, it would not be possible to prepare one complete list of best practices/tools comprising the different methodological techniques that a Physical Education teacher should use. Instead, we provide examples of practices/tools that can be labelled as social pedagogic and encourage Physical Education teachers to apply and/or adjust them to their circumstances.

Practice One: Planning Curriculum and Instruction within a Co-constructed Classroom Space

Many physical educators feel more secure with carrying out the purely practical part of their work. However, social pedagogic work in Physical Education needs to be planned and organised systematically in separate stages of instructional planning. For this purpose, the Physical Education teacher may begin by defining the situation (*what is happening in the classroom*), continue by formulating the goals of work to be done (*how do we proceed to enact change about what is happening*), plan a subsequent curriculum/activity (*what needs to be done in practice*) and ultimately evaluate the results of this work (*what have we accomplished, what needs to be added or changed*). Social pedagogic work is often experienced as a circular process, where the different stages are illustrated as discrete and interrelated circles, with the last circle being not only the 'last stage', but also the 'first stage' in the next round of the social pedagogic work. The teacher aims to help students stretch their development zone by moving from their comfort to their learning zone without entering a panic zone.

Table 2.1 Social pedagogy tools for Physical Education practice

Social pedagogy tool	Explanation
Curriculum planning	Professional planning and documentation for activity implementation and evaluation
Language used within the lesson	Specialist language as an expression of knowledge and practice in the field Use of pedagogic conversations and dialogues within classroom activities
Group work	Working with groups rather than teams of students. Group life and its associative logic is important for lesson design The content selected by the teacher focuses on activation work done and decided together with students
Lesson concepts	*Cooperation*: Sharing with others, helping, following rules, dealing with messages *Self-Assertion*: Asking for information, presenting one's view, reacting *Self-Control*: Ability to wait turns, compromise and react appropriately *Empathy*: Showing consideration and respect for others' feelings and opinions *Responsibility*: Communicating, showing respect to work and property *Conflict negotiation and boundary setting*: Activities with a focus on correcting perspectives
Teaching Methods	*Get to know conversations*. These conversations focus on getting people together before engaging in common activities *Glimmers of Good Performance*. All students are treated as valued human beings, and they have moments of positive performance/behaviour. These moments are praised by the teacher *Quick return to structure*. The teachers have a structure for their interventions to which they return together with students *Talk little messages*. Instructions/feedback being kept simple and explicit

Practice Two: Pedagogic Conversations to Enable Closeness

Within social pedagogy, language is fundamental for enacting dialogue that can help youth to weigh up the pros and cons of their actions and address their dilemmas with reflection. Usually, pedagogic conversations occur in the social space constructed when pedagogues and students have found ways to act together relationally. Within this space, the teacher needs to be able both to stay close to students and understand their situation from a professional standpoint to help them enact change. Let's take the hypothetical example of a secondary school student who feels uncomfortable working with other students during a Physical Education lesson. From a social pedagogic perspective, it would not be enough for the Physical Education teacher to say, "…I can understand what you are going through. Please tell me how you feel...". Even though such a use of language conveys empathetic understanding, it is not adequate for promoting change. The next step for the Physical Education teacher would be to analyse what is happening with this student and refer to strategies/methods that could provide a solution. This is where the use of specialist language would come in:

> ... I think that it is important that you start spending time with other students during recess, to be part of the student community and learn more about them. That way, you may find it easier to make new friends and feel comfortable working with others...

As physical educators, it is important that we make observations, not judgements, in our dialogue with students. Sometimes, we rush to 'rescue' a student from an unpleasant situation without first helping the student to observe what is happening and reflect on his/her actions. Within social pedagogic conversations, such observations need to be factual. The absence of judgements and threats and their replacement with mild-mannered and positive suggestions is very important for the success of all social pedagogic conversations (i.e., see an example of a mild-mannered suggestion in the opening vignette). The following excerpt is also an example of a factual observation conversation that a Physical Education teacher can have with a student to shed attention to shared classroom experiences:

> ...John, please look at Mary. Now that you have stepped in and taken her place in the game, how does she seem to feel?? Do you think she's annoyed? Do you agree that it is a good idea for both of you if you apologised and let her play at her turn next time?

Practice Three: Group-Oriented Work

Group-oriented work is essential for social pedagogic interventions since it helps children and youth learn about social life while collaborating within games and leisure-oriented activities. The teacher's role in group activities is facilitating action and conflict negotiation to safeguard change-oriented work. Compared to other forms of group-oriented teaching, social pedagogic teaching does not arrange games and activities, leaving students to play. Instead, the teachers physically relocate themselves, go where students are, and work with them in these games/activities. Their purpose is to listen to students' arguments and help them practice their ability to negotiate and resolve conflicts by teaching them about the 'classroom culture' in which they both live. To do so, teachers may use a variety of techniques, such as *confrontational learning* (Storø, 2013) (i.e., the teacher grasps the unpleasantness of a situation and helps the students confront it with a learning effect that could reduce or prevent repetition), or *boundary-setting* (i.e., the teacher helps the students understand the difference between right and wrong). In these techniques, the teacher tries to find *a balance between correction and acknowledgement* to help the students manage similar circumstances in the future on their own. The vignette at the beginning of this chapter gives examples of both techniques. Teachers need to be able to take the other's perspective in each situation to be able to work with consideration to children's and youth's physical and emotional aspects of their (shared) life spaces (Cameron et al., 2021). Caring, honesty, assertiveness, perspective-taking, conflict negotiation, emotional support, respect, and planning are some concepts that could be used as overarching elements of group work.

Key Points

- In social pedagogy teachers work with children and youth by sharing a life space of co-constructed activities
- Pedagogic dialogues enable reflection and group work

Advice from the Field

Amelie Debbouze (France, Physical Education Teacher Education)

The professional, the personal, and private self of the Physical Education teacher are always in a constant interaction and negotiation during teaching. I always keep notes in my reflection journal at the end of each class. I want to be explicit about what went well and what not. This is part of my professional attitude as a teacher. The last few days I am working with students on a modern dance unit and communication in pairs is important. In every lesson, I use personal examples, I talk about my years in high school and that teacher who inspired me to follow a career in dance. By talking about me, I find the opportunity to learn also more about my students. I want them to feel liked for what they are and what they can achieve. Some of them feel so desperate to compete and there are others who are still very shy. My private self would want to go in front of the class and perform that dance routine with poise and flow. I want to show them what a competent dancer I am. But if I allowed my private self to do that my professionally established goals for this group of students would be undermined. I want everyone to experience success for what they can achieve. So, I keep myself at the background of the class and work with all of them, guiding their discovery of movements. I do so until I sense that they are engaged in what we are doing both as a group and individually. I know that at the end of the semester, I will be very proud of everyone.

Summary

Social pedagogy aims to develop each person's ability and competence to thrive in their life. In Chapter 2, we presented basic principles and practices for working with social pedagogy in Physical Education. Our goal was to inform Physical Education teachers about how they can work with youth via social pedagogy to help them commit to change and progress. We described the change as mainly relational, permanently residing in all those bottom-up activities or practices that the Physical Education teacher may use to create shared spaces of commonly decided group work. Stage-by-stage instructional planning, use of specialist pedagogic language and opportunities for group reflection were suggested as tools needed to support social pedagogic work in Physical Education.

Reflection Questions and Activities

1. What does it mean to live as a child or young person within modern societies?
2. How do we perceive care and pedagogic work in today's Physical Education classrooms?
3. How could you describe the Physical Education profession as a form of education based on relationships?
4. What kind of relationships are most important for you as a professional?

Note

1. In German literature, *Bildung* is a concept that refers to education as a process of enculturation, character formation, and emotional and moral development, all of which support lifelong learning that forces students to grow and change.

References

Cameron, C., Moss, P. & Petrie, P. (2021). Towards a social pedagogic approach for social care. *International Journal of Social Pedagogy*, *10*(1), 7. https://doi.org/10.14324/111.444.ijsp.2021.v10.x.007

Dall'Alba, G., & Barnacle, R. (2007). An ontological turn for higher education. *Studies in Higher Education*, *32*, 679–691. https://doi.org/10.1080/03075070701685130

Eichsteller, G., & Holthoff, S. (2012). The art of being a social pedagogue: Developing cultural change in children's homes in Essex. *International Journal of Social Pedagogy*, *1*(1), 30–46. Retrieved from http://www.internationaljournalofsocialpedagogy.com

Storø, J. (2013). *Practical social pedagogy: Theories, values and tools for working with children and young people*. Policy Press.

Additional Resources

Colton, M., Sanders, R., & Williams, M. (2017). *An introduction to working with children: A guide for social workers*. Bloomsbury Publishing.

Davies, M. (Ed.). (2013). *The Blackwell companion to social work*. John Wiley & Sons.

Part II
Strategies for Supporting Practitioners to Use Social Pedagogy in Physical Education

3 A Multidisciplinary Approach to Social Pedagogy

A Pedagogical Case

Cláudio Farias

Learning Objectives

At the end of this chapter you will be able to:

- Appreciate the importance of social pedagogy to improve the social inclusion of children (especially minority groups such as Newcomer Immigrant Children).
- Understand how the principles of social pedagogy can be expressed in a multidisciplinary approach to social inclusion.

VIGNETTE: An Ontological View on the Social Pedagogical Case

I (Ferreira-dos-Santos) am a white male professor and researcher interested in transdisciplinary research and social pedagogy practice. I often resort to theories, models and frameworks within the sociology, pedagogy, psychology, and philosophy disciplines. I have worked mainly as a coach and teacher-candidates developer and have been a sports coach for the last ten years, trying to create more socially just environments for youth participants.

My contribution in this pedagogical case is the call for clarification, at the onset, of the ontological perspective that will guide the project (one that all contributing disciplines should consider). This will help to shape the tone of our professional and interpersonal interactions, understand how we perceive the world, if and what we deem "right and wrong" (if such distinction ever exists), and why we think (and exist in the world) and act in this pedagogical case the way we do; hopefully, in a manner consistent with social pedagogy principles.

I advocate for moving beyond a deficit approach to social interventions. When we think of the inclusion of minorities as facilitated by mentoring activities (from an experienced teacher, from preservice teachers and their mediating university supervisors, or even as students who are invested in mentoring their Newcomer Immigrant Children (NIC) peers), we should counter the "instinct" of positioning development, learning and educational objectives through a deficit approach (Camiré et al., 2023). This may locate immigrant children as incomplete beings, ever unable to contribute and fulfil neoliberal standards and, thus, in need of "being fixed" to fit in. Although it may seem paradoxical, I would also advise that in working for the social inclusion of NIC we shouldn't expect, unrealistically, that it doesn't require some "compromise" on their part. Their school peers will always expect that they exhibit certain habits and attitudes that identify them as "one of our mates". In finding a balance, it is up to all contributors to safeguard, above all, NIC's right to their identity, their Self and universally recognised right to be accepted (and valued) in the school community for the unique human beings they are. Thus, accessing children's and youth's ontologies represents a needed strategy to increase understanding and foster meaningful development through participation in Physical Education and sports (recognising multiple worlds; Snaza & Weaver, 2015).

Introductory Note

I would like to point out from the outset that all the experts contributing to this pedagogical case (active or retired) are real people who work (or have worked) in real institutions and who are currently actively involved in drawing up this social intervention project.

Introduction: Pedagogical Cases

A "Pedagogical case", as coined by Kathleen Armour (2017), represents a professional intervention mechanism in education capable of bringing together multidisciplinary teams to assist practitioners' professional action and improve children's and youth's lives. A pedagogical case aims to deeply understand and participate in the educational experiences or social conditions in which an individual learner (a Physical Education student) or a group of learners (a specific population within a school) are situated (Casey et al., 2017).

A multidisciplinary team of academics and professionals is brought together to improve social pedagogy practice's design, delivery, and effectiveness. The goal is to provide the main actors in the pedagogical case with social and emotional tools, empowering them to take control of their lives and enhance their social inclusion and overall well-being. Based on each specialist's unique perspectives, singular expertise, and cutting-edge knowledge in their respective fields, a research-theory-practice bridge is established, as each team member contributes to enriching the pedagogical case.

A Multidisciplinary Approach to Social Pedagogy 35

The pedagogical case process includes: a) Constructing the case narrative as a description of the focal learner or learners; (b) drawing on insights by academic and practitioner experts from at least three different disciplines (in and beyond kinesiology) to analyse the educational needs of that young person or youth group; (c) crafting a plan of action with the participation of all specialists, who strive to uncover the most effective state-of-the-art knowledge from their fields that could aid the intervention and enrich the participants' experience; (d) a contribution is provided, summarising key evidence from each expert's field; and (e) a narrative is provided as a way to reach out to teachers and inspire them with confidence to learn, help them to change practice, and provide them with a language for sharing their learning.

The "Social Pedagogical" Case: Social Inclusion of Newcomer Immigrant Children in the School Community through Physical Education and Sport Participation

Most pedagogical cases typically involve ongoing or completed pedagogical-investigative projects. The case we present is still in the "design" phase, preparing for implementation in the next school year. The specialist intervention focuses on the most significant structural aspects to consider when developing the project without reporting on eventual yet-unlived constraints and challenges.

Background and Purpose

Like many countries, Portugal is experiencing a remarkably fast-moving wave of (im)migration. Government bodies and social institutions nationwide, particularly schools, are grappling with restructuring their internal functional structures while trying to welcome and integrate Newcomer Immigrant Children (NIC) into the community.

However, recent research suggests that the community integration of NIC may be hindered by cultural, language, ethnic, or religious barriers. There are reported cases of social exclusion of NIC, negatively impacting their well-being and self-esteem (Huxhold et al., 2022). The lack of educational interventions to deliberately facilitate the social inclusion of NIC has aggravated this situation, primarily due to a lack of coordinated plans among teachers from different curriculum disciplines within the school to promote the social inclusion of NIC. Inadequate coordination between school services and other relevant services, such as social care services, is also missing. Such coordination is critical as proper action demands an integral comprehension of the circumstances in which NIC leave their daily lives. Namely, including their family in the inclusion endeavour. Therefore, the pedagogical case presented here aims *to create an intervention plan to expedite the social inclusion of NIC in the school community*. In light of social pedagogy tenets, the participation of NIC in Physical Education classes and extracurricular sessions of sports-based activities is proposed to "accelerate" their social inclusion.

The School Community

The intervention context is an urban school in northern Portugal with approximately 2,300 students. Among these are approximately 700 immigrant students from over 25 nationalities. The "influx" of NIC into the school has been particularly notable in recent years, with an average of 40 children and youth entering this school each year in the last three years.

The host school stands out for welcoming preservice teachers (PSTs) from multiple disciplines to conduct their school placement training, benefiting from a wide range of recognised teaching expertise from cooperating teachers. The school is quite receptive to implementing innovative social-driven pedagogical projects, frequently shaped by multiple community activities led by the Physical Education group. Typically, an average of ten preservice teachers are placed in the host school every year, and they take on significant responsibility in energising the intervention in the school community beyond the Physical Education lessons.

The Social Pedagogy Educational Intervention

In taking a broadened understanding of sport and participation in sport (see below "Sport contribution to social pedagogy"), the participation of NIC in socially inclusive Physical Education classes and extracurricular sport-based activities will be used as a social inclusion "accelerator" (Carter-Thuillier et al., 2018).

First, both *Physical Education classes* and the *extracurricular sports activities* will be taught in an autonomy-supportive approach (see below "A curriculum contribution") known to facilitate students' social development, promote increased social bonds within and beyond the classroom, and generate more inclusive and equitable learning experiences to all students.

Second, *Physical Education PSTs* will be empowered as prime active educational and social transformation agents. This pedagogical case will expand their role as teachers beyond "content delivery" in Physical Education lessons towards becoming more fully participative members of the educational community. The PSTs are expected to go beyond what Ferreira-dos-Santos reports as a 'deficit approach' (see vignette at the beginning of this chapter) and become active mediators of the networking established between the school and other relevant social agents (social workers, school psychologists, and teachers from various subjects like English, Portuguese, or Arts) that will steer the social inclusion of NIC. In other words, the PSTs become *social pedagogues*.

Tying the Dots Together: The Multidisciplinary Social Pedagogy Approach

In this pedagogical case, the structuring principle of social pedagogy is its aspiration to ensure every individual's right to dignity and preserve their cultural identity, especially in contexts where their characteristics may be seen as divergent from the norm, as indicative of diversity. We gather the perspectives of five specialists in a collaborative effort to promote social inclusion for NIC. A humanistic ontological positioning, a sport pedagogy, a Physical Education curriculum, a Physical Education teacher education (PETE), a sport sociology, and a social service perspective were assembled.

Table 3.1 summarises the points of interaction and complementarity between the foundational principles of social pedagogy considered in this book and the facets of the multidisciplinary contribution. For the Sport, Curriculum and PETE contributions, we show how each of the elements of the proposals is aligned with particular social pedagogy principles. The Ontology, Sports Sociology, and Social Service dimensions are transversal to the process, for they are "vigilant" of the humanistic values that ethically inform all contributions. While aligning with The Common Third and The Diamond Model, the sport sociology themes "ethics of care" and "diversity as cultural richness" are teaching material in the curriculum (e.g., during socially oriented group discussions: content-embedded pro-social development). In addition, the "multi-systemic integrated approach" afforded by the social service perspective provides the team with an augmented understanding of the family circumstances in which NIC live and a broader understanding of children's responses to the proposed activities.

Figure 3.1 presents a schematic representation of the pedagogical case's interactive structure. We highlight the role of the PSTs as leading social agents in NIC's social inclusion and the support networks that will emerge to enact their socio-pedagogical action collaboratively. PSTs' intervention is supported by school-based (cooperating teachers' mediation) and PETE mentoring (university supervisor). Networking is established with other educational agents in the school (e.g., the class director who contacts the NIC families) and with social services, while the curriculum proposal shapes the use of sport as a cultural artefact to enact a social pedagogical approach to Physical Education and sport participation.

Sport Contribution to Social Pedagogy

Zelia is a recently retired professor who worked for over 30 years at a Portuguese sport faculty. Sport pedagogy as a scientific discipline has always been her topic of interest. In teacher training (Physical Education and sport), it was the motto for deepening the "pedagogical competence" theme, which translated into her active role in designing professional practicum and teacher

Table 3.1 Interconnection between social pedagogy principles and multidisciplinary contributions

Social pedagogy principles	Multidisciplinary contribution					
	Ontology	Sport (cultural theme)	Curriculum	PETE	Sociology	Social work
The Common Third	Accessing children's ontologies	Movement sub-cultures	Peer-mentoring	Human-centred mentoring		
Head – Heart – Hands	Ontological clarification of action	Integrative values Education through movement	Autonomy-supportive experiences Phased scaffolding of embodied social responsibility			Multi-systemic approach First-hand witnessing
Participation Preparing for participation	Collaborative transformation commitment	Learning pluralism	Socially responsible decision-making	Community immersion	Ethics of Care	Ongoing programme assessment
The Diamond Model	Children's empowerment Strengths-based, co-constructed	Self and group identity Emancipatory social action	Content-embedded pro-social development Multidimensional	Tailor-made professional development	Social bias de-construction Diversity as cultural richness Peer-caring	Multiple institutional networking
Creativity	ontology and intervention	Alternative social dimension Education in movement	tailor-made teaching and assessment	Liaising (institutional) skills and social-oriented action		Family independence
The three Ps						

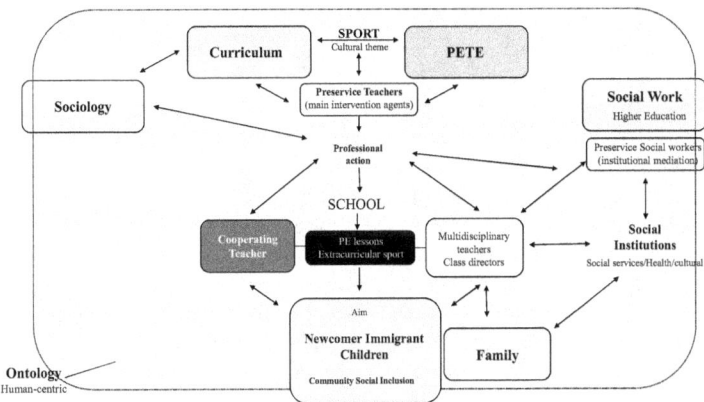

Figure 3.1 The social pedagogical case.

education curriculum. She is mentoring emerging newcomer academics and passing on the institution's axiological identity.

I conceive of the learner as anyone who practises sport in any context in which that practice occurs. It derives from an understanding of Sport Pedagogy that broadly and comprehensively views sport while integrating various movement subcultures. It considers education in both a broad and strict sense. Thus, all sport practice warrants and deserves a pedagogical clarification, harnessing the full educative potential of sport and meeting the profound demands of human education. A Physical Education student is just as much a sport participant as a player in a sports club, as is the child who plays and practises sport in more informal settings such as the school playground, extracurricular activities, or a social institution.

Sport Pluralism and Movement Subcultures

The perspective of sport I present here includes all bodily exercises and all games and forms of exercise, oriented by movement, practised with or without regularity, aimed at high performance or recreation and leisure, practised in any institution: club, school, gyms, or in any social institutional context (Grupe & Krüger, 1994).

On the Pedagogical Value of Sport: What Use Is It for Social Pedagogy?

Part of the richness of sport stems from the diversity of effects it generates and, consequently, from the plurality of objectives it can help different populations who practise sport to achieve. Possible effects of practising sport include: somatic (strengthening muscles and organs), motor (improving conditional and coordinative skills, learning specific skills), sensory (improving the sense of perception), emotional (learning to live, master and enjoy feelings), motivational (providing interests, stimulating and developing new motivations), cognitive (building motor images and acquiring practical knowledge) and social (experimenting with group socialisation, in the form of cooperation and competition) (Matos, 1999).

Therefore, sport participation can be used as specific social work at the service of inclusion and integration because it offers numerous opportunities for social development: training social skills, practising teamwork, experiencing fair play (honesty, a sense of justice, contributing to justice-inclusion), equality, reducing prejudice, the opportunity to build meaning, personal commitment, and dedication, strengthening contacts, possibly also contributing to social integration, international understanding or reconciliation. When social development happens due to individuals' engagement in sport-based movement experiences (expressed by learners' development of communication skills, social interaction abilities, pro-social behaviour, and conflict resolution skills), *social pedagogy outcomes emerge.*

Sport, Culture, and Social Belonging

Sport is intrinsically cultural because it contains principles, values, attitudes, relationships, norms, rules, obligations, duties, conflicts, challenges, demands, ideals, goals, creations, and achievements. This gives it a scalable nature (with tangible outcomes), with patterns of behaviour clearly associated with it; sport "speaks" a universal language. There is a body of knowledge that tells us what to do and why. The NIC, or any other participant in a sport, knows if they have become faster than they were, if they have become more psychologically focused on the task and if they are collaborative team players. Such achievement informs others about the person's value because this results from the practitioner's effort and ability, which must be conquered and maintained daily through persistent and systematic work. For example, establishing synchronisation of movement and creating a common language with the other person so that, for example, they can play together shows evidence of the learner's commitment to learning the "social capital" of that community; their commitment towards belonging to the community. In short, sport participation, such as in Physical Education lessons, extracurricular sports-based activities, or sports clubs, *creates an opportunity to belong to a specific world of a specific sports language.*

A Curriculum Contribution

Cláudio *is a professor in Sport Pedagogy. He works in teacher and coach education and maintains a very close relationship with schools through* *regular partnerships in research and social-pedagogical interventions. He is passionate about Physical Education, teaching, and learning. He will present two contributions suggesting an integrative human-centred/ learner-oriented/social pedagogy approach to the Physical Education curriculum and PETE.*

A Social Pedagogy Approach to Physical Education and Sport Participation

The educational value of implementing a social pedagogy approach in Physical Education is self-explanatory. Nonetheless, Physical Education is a mandatory subject in the school curriculum and requires careful and informed consideration by social pedagogues. It holds a unique subject-matter as it is the only subject in the curriculum to educate through, by and in the movement. Sports, exercise, and games are far too important in human (and educational) culture to remain underdeveloped as mere "social entertainment". Therefore, a social pedagogy approach must consider several educational "tasks" demanded of Physical education (e.g., students must evidence discipline-specific knowledge and skills). Thus, teachers and students are held accountable for efficient teaching and successful learning. Also, the assessment and grading of students directly impact their lives. The cumulative assessment average gathered during secondary education is considered in the application to higher education. As suggested early at the beginning of this chapter (see opening vignette), it is important for Physical Education teachers to reflect on how they perceive the world and why they think and act in one way instead of another. How social pedagogy can take shape in Physical Education, while informed by social pedagogy principles, needs some level of curriculum clarification, which I offer here.

Foundational Educational Objectives

Every learning and human development in sport participation is shaped by and within social interactions. I suggest the learner-oriented, human-centred approach proposed by Farias and Mesquita (2022) as an operational means of realising social pedagogy goals. This builds on the foundational assertion that productive instructional interactions (teacher-student/student-student) are viable if the nature and quality of the social relationships that mediate that learning are built on respectful, socially empathetic, collaborative interactions. *Work with*, rather *than for* the child is pursued as we seek the highest development of the learner (multidimensional: motor, cognitive, social, and affective outcomes) with their most active involvement in the process; students take self-determined responsibility for their own development and that of their peers.

Foundational Social Pedagogies

The curriculum operations include extensive engagement in peer-assisted learning and self- and peer-assessment, collaborative and discovery-learning activities, and extensive participation in content-embedded pro-social critical group reflection. These interactions are tailored for social development and awareness (inclusive attitudes, acceptance of difference, social empathy) and for the progressive transfer of decision-making power to learners with increasing ownership of the learning experience (learning how to learn and teach each other sport, games, and positive social attitudes).

When students are tasked to invest in the collaborative achievement of common goals and mentor their peers, they implicitly demonstrate care and concern for each other. Sharing knowledge on motor skills, peer-guidance on how to behave as a group member and safely prompting students' manifestations of feelings lead to embodied group identities, positive self-critical thinking, and a sense of belonging. As social bonds are tightened, learners become more sensitive to peers' diverse strengths and learning needs, regardless of their ability level or socio-cultural background (Luguetti et al., 2017). Thus, it becomes easier to escape deficit forms of thinking – as stated within the vignette at the beginning of this chapter – which treat children as incomplete beings, always in need of "being fixed" to fit in.

Teaching, Learning, and Assessment

Ultimately, instead of fitting students into the norm, this learner-oriented social perspective adapts the norm to each individual student through (a) individualised task demands allowing students with different levels of ability to be included in the same learning situation, (b) by teaching, assessing, and acknowledging multidimensional strengths (specially peer-leadership or inclusive game-play attitudes), and, (c) by applying tailor-made, dynamic, self-referenced, responsive, and dynamic assessment (Farias et al., 2020).

A Physical Education Teacher Education Perspective

The prospective teachers (PSTs) will be the primary mediating agents of NIC's social inclusion in the school community. Consequently, PSTs are called to embody a broad understanding of what being a teacher means, as strongly imbued by a professional social pedagogy approach. This implies building a web of mediation layers to support PSTs' intervention (MacPhail & Tannehill, 2012). The PSTs' interventions, as mentored by Cooperating teachers (CTs) will benefit from a close collaboration between the school and university. The CTs must facilitate PSTs' immersion in the school community. The legitimacy of PSTs as full-fledged members of the professional teaching community (students, fellow teachers, and social workers) will grow and "open doors" to their educational action.

Humanising the Mentoring Process

Adjusting the mentoring provided by CTs to the individual characteristics of each PST involves understanding their socio-economic context, negotiating collective and individual goals, and facilitating their access to resources like free school meals or printing allowances.

Mediating Proximal Networking

PSTs are typically placed in groups. This creates opportunities for professional development and social interaction within and as a *community of practice*. Activating group identity among PSTs, structuring deliberate cooperative work for task completion, and enhancing group cohesion is achievable by drawing on each PST's strengths (e.g., each PST leads the group planning in the teaching units they are most knowledgeable of).

Pedagogical Intervention Mediation

The teacher educators, including the university supervisor, continuously support PSTs' pedagogical and social intervention. I highlight four processes (Farias et al., 2023).

Cyclical and Responsive Support

Iterative action should be in place with (a) weekly work sessions at the university with the PSTs focused on discussing their ongoing day-to-day needs, (b) followed by expert pedagogical suggestions on how to help address their fears and struggles, and (c) suggesting possible intervention strategies if requested.

Multidimensional Assessment of Professional Practice

Given the expectation that PSTs develop a broad-spectrum professional practice, assessing such professional practice should encourage their investment in relationship building and participation with the school community (and beyond). The PETE programme can establish the following evaluative dimensions: (i) Knowing (mobilises knowledge needed to promote socially and personally meaningful learning for students); (ii) acting (generates a climate that contributes to student motivation and participation in positive, equitable and inclusive social relationships); (iii) reflecting (is self-critical and learns from personal (and with) others' experience); (iv) socialising (establishes positive social relationships with the community and beyond).

A Sport Sociology Contribution

Luisa *is a sports sociologist at a university in northern Portugal. She is qualified in Physical Education teaching and has developed an academic focus on Sport's philosophical, Religious, and Cultural facets. She has led various projects with the Portuguese Olympic Committee and county-wide intervention programs for female sports participation.*

(Im)migration Brings New Challenges

Several considerations come to mind when establishing how sport sociology can aid social pedagogy. Strongly driven by war, migration flows have increased significantly in Ukraine and the Middle East. This poses challenges to the organisation of social life in host countries. Promoting knowledge and respect for customs and traditions is crucial for (im)migrant and host countries' citizens.

Philosophical Aids

There are no ready-made recipes for integrating NIC in the educational community. I highlight the need to embrace inclusion by considering various philosophical perspectives of ethics. Virtue ethics, duty ethics (or deontological), consequentialist ethics (MacIntyre, 2016) and, the ethics of care. This is critical in our pedagogical case because there is no true inclusion without developing empathy and mutual responsibility, beyond any general or abstract social rule.

The ethics of care implies reconciling the peaceful coexistence of diverse people with diverse cultures and understandings of social life and, at the same time, their interdependence. Our native teenagers are unaware that we are a nation historically shaped by emigration. It is crucial to deconstruct specific cultural "forces" fading the dichotomy between "us" and "others". I suggest fostering curiosity and sharing some of the cultural customs that may manifest more concretely in classes. Some examples in Physical Education include creating a forum for traditional sports practices from NIC's original countries or understanding the impact of religious beliefs on their predisposition to activities (from issues of sacred calendar to dietary or clothing habits).

Diversity

Multiculturalism and diversity are, according to UNESCO, social wealth benchmarks. However, a paradox arises in globalisation, where diversity can be compromised or "infringed" with a tendency towards homogenisation.

Globalisation may tend to promote similar behavioural trends. This highlights the need to raise awareness among participants about emerging primitive human reactions that must be fought to embrace instead what is initially dimmed differently but, with time, becomes social wealth.

Time, Belonging and Peer-Caring

Belonging is a relentless pursuit of human beings; especially for NIC and their families. We are "desiring machines", seeking to dedicate our time to meaningful interactions. Time is scarce, luxurious, and precious. Peer-mentoring activities, based on humanised social relationships, are an excellent way to promote awareness of the social wealth that emerges when we put our time at the service of others. The exchange of knowledge about games or physical movements between peer-mentors and mentees intrinsically contains affection and a caring look towards the other. Such caring embeds the will to empower and "free" the person towards further action in the social world and community participation. I advise that we consider youngsters and their circumstances by seeking to understand their family life.

A Social Service Contribution

Etelvina is a social worker with over three decades of experience. She has worked in schools and hospitals with different populations. She was the coordinator of the Social Action Service and has carried out significant work in the Pediatrics Service for 25 years. She has participated in multidisciplinary working groups in healthcare, was a speaker at seminars, and supervised social work students' professional placement for nearly two decades.

A Social Worker's Positioning

As a social service worker, my primary concern is understanding why this NIC community chose this country. Many immigrants seek refuge from war or violence, while others pursue economic survival and dignity. Language barriers, especially for those from non-Portuguese-speaking countries, pose critical challenges to their integration. In the case of immigrants from Brazil or the PALOP[1] countries, language will be a less complicated barrier to overcome. Yet, if the NIC doesn't speak our language, it's imperative to find ways of facilitating their inclusion.

Social Service

The social work professional approach aims to promote positive change in society, impacting the lives of individuals, families, and communities. It responds to the families' everyday struggles through counselling, case management, group, and educational work, and helping people obtain vital goods and services in the community. We help them develop their full potential, enrich their lives, and alleviate any limitations or barriers to a dignifying human condition (Harrikari & Rauhala, 2016).

An Integrated Approach

The NIC phenomenon must be seen from an integrated perspective. Knowing the child one-on-one is essential. Yet, social service focuses on the child but works with the NIC family (Garcia, 2009). If the family lacks harmony, the child is not well. We must contact the child's parents and/or other significant family members to understand the family and its social context.

Social Service Methodology

There are four main steps to follow. The *Study and Social Diagnosis* accesses the socio-economic context, housing conditions, health, and the relationships established among various family members. Home visits, e.g., outside of regular working hours, allow for *first-hand witnessing*. Observing family dynamics and the NIC in their daily reality helps us to identify the most pressing needs (lack of housing or employment, health problems, socio-economic precariousness, and food shortages) to individualise the action plan. This facilitates coordination with institutions best equipped to address these needs. The *Planning and intervention* are fundamentally a "social service liaising intervention". It involves individualised monitoring of families and liaison with the community institutions to whom a previously prepared "social report" should be addressed. The *Appraisal of the social service* is critical: whether it worked or not, what worked and didn't work, why, what could have been done differently, and what implications for future cases. Finally, *Independence, self-regulation, and open channels* are achieved when the social worker steers families to the services that can best help them and scaffold their way towards independence. The aim is to ensure the family's livelihood and self-management before fading the "intervention". Families learn about the services' location, people, and procedures and can seek them out directly in the future. The "file" remains open, and we'll be around to help.

Social Service Liaising Intervention

Social workers must comprehensively map all institutions available within the community. It is critical to grasp the system's functioning and how various institutions are interconnected, as this enhances our capacity to assist families (Tadic et al., 2020).

Healthcare

If a child or family member faces complex health issues, it is essential to gather all relevant information, include a medical report in the process, develop an appropriate action plan, and collaborate with other services and contexts (National Health Service).

School

Collaboration with the school is one of the most critical means of intervention. The social worker establishes a professional relationship with the school psychologist, the resident social worker, and the Physical Education staff to mediate their interactions with Social Action Services or the Local Health Units. If the NIC are not fluent in the host country's language, it is crucial to collaborate with the school to offer additional classes in the native language. The school can contact Social Services to find out about the children's living conditions and their impact on school performance, or the Social Services can liaise with class directors to contextualise the situation of children in the school.

Higher Education

There are thousands of NIC and their families on the move. However, social work requires an individualised approach, and there is a limit to the number of cases that can be dealt with by a single social worker. Thus, a team of social workers is needed. Building partnerships with higher education institutions and training new professionals is a way to achieve this. Integrating in-training social workers in social work school placement will allow them to reach out to all NIC families, which requires collaboration with higher education professors and social work school placement supervisors.

Summary

We offered a pedagogical case seeking the inclusion of a minority population (NIC). This calls for a social pedagogy that guides good practice and educational intervention to protect human dignity beyond notions of children as incomplete beings (see introductory vignette). In addition, the participation of children and young people in human-centred Physical Education and school sports activities provides for the educational realisation of social pedagogy. Social pedagogy in action entails complementary articulation of various disciplines that connect theory and practice.

Reflection Questions and Activities

1 Reflect on the NIC phenomenon in your context (country) and try to outline what your current role is in the social inclusion of these children and

young people; if you are not satisfied with this role, what are you going to do about it?
2 Consider what your contribution could be to the application of a pedagogical case in your professional context and what possible partners could contribute to this intervention.

Note

1 Portuguese-speaking African Countries.

References

Armour, K.M. (2017). Pedagogical cases: A new translational mechanism to bridge theory/research practice gaps in youth physical activity education (PAE). *Kinesiology Review*, 6(1), 42–50. https://doi.org/10.1123/kr.2016-0037
Camiré, M., Santos, F., Newman, T., Vella, S., MacDonald, D.J., Milistetd, M., Pierce, S., & Strachan, L. (2023). Positive youth development as a guiding framework in sport research: Is it time to plan for a transition? *Psychology of Sport & Exercise*, 69, 1–8. https://doi.org/10.1016/j.psychsport.2023.102505
Carter-Thuillier, B., López-Pastor, V., Gallardo-Fuentes, F., & Carter-Beltran, J. (2018). Immigration and social inclusion: Possibilities from school and sports. In Tiago Sequeira (Ed.), *Immigration and Development*. pp. 57–74 London: Intechopen. http://dx.doi.org/10.5772/intechopen.72028
Casey, A., Goodyear, V.A., & Armour, K.M. (2017). *Digital technologies and learning in physical education*. Routledge.
Farias, C., Fernández-Río, J., Martins, J., Ribeiro, E., Teixeira, J., Bessa, C., & Mesquita, I. (2023). Multi-system influences on physical education preservice teachers' teaching practice in pandemic times. *Quest*, 75(4), 325–343. https://doi.org/10.1080/00336297.2023.2189130
Farias, C., & Mesquita, I. (2022). *Learner-oriented teaching and assessment in youth sport*, Routledge, MiniBook series. Routledge. (ISBN 9780367690076)
Farias, C., Wallhead, T., & Mesquita, I. (2020). "The project changed my life": Sport education's transformative potential on student physical literacy. *Research Quarterly for Exercise and Sport*, 91(2), 263–278. https://doi.org/10.1080/02701367.2019.1661948
Garcia, B. (2009). Theory and social work practice with immigrant populations. In Fernando Chang-Muy and Elaine Congress (2nd Ed.) New York: Springer publishing company. *Social work with immigrants and refugees: Legal issues, clinical skills, and advocacy* (pp. 79–102). https://doi.org/10.1891/9780826126696.0004
Grupe, O. & Krüger, M. (1994). Sport pedagogy. The anthropological approach. *Sport Science Review*, 3(1) 18–27.
Harrikari, T., & Rauhala, P.L. (2016). *Social change and social work: The changing societal conditions of social work in time and place*. Routledge.
Huxhold, O., Suanet, B., & Wetzel, M. (2022). Perceived social exclusion and loneliness: Two distinct but related phenomena. *Sociological Science*, 9, 430–453. https://doi.org/10.15195/v9.a17
Luguetti, C., Oliver, K.L., Kirk, D., & Dantas, L. (2017). Exploring an activist approach of working with boys from socially vulnerable backgrounds in a sport context. *Sport*,

Education and Society, 22(4), 493–510. https://doi.org/10.1080/13573322.2015.10542 74

MacIntyre, A. (2016). *The irrelevance of ethics*. Routledge.

MacPhail, A., & Tannehill, D. (2012). Helping preservice and beginning teachers examine and reframe assumptions about themselves as teachers and change agents: "Who is going to listen to you anyway?". *Quest, 64*(4), 299–312. https://doi.org/10.1080/00336297.2012.706885

Matos, Z. (1999). *Estudo da pedagogia do desporto em Portugal: contributo para a sua compreensão*. Tese de doutoramento em Ciências do Desporto e Educação Física (Ciências do Desporto) apresentada à Fac. de Ciências do Desporto e Educação Física de Coimbra.

Snaza, N., & Weaver, J. (2015). *Posthumanism and educational research*. Routledge.

Tadic, V., Ashcroft, R., Brown, J.B., & Dahrouge, S. (2020). The role of social workers in interprofessional primary healthcare teams. *Healthcare Policy, 16*(1), 27–42. https://doi.org/10.12927/hcpol.2020.26292

Additional Resources

Webinar series – TGfU 40th anniversary: https://www.google.com/search?client= safari&rls=en&q=Webinar+2%3A+Learner+oriented+Instructional+and+social+ scaffolding+in+GBAs&ie=UTF-8&oe=UTF-8#fpstate=ive&vld=cid:1561049b, vid:pIOPMaPvpGY,st:0

4 The Syn-Epistemic Wholeness of Physical Education Practice

Zack Beddoes and Emily Jones

Learning Objectives

At the end of this chapter, you will be able to:

- Understand how a systems perspective can provide a pathway for building collective action formations that enhance access to resources and experiences that empower students in Physical Education.
- Understand aspects that are necessary for Physical Education teacher education (PETE) and school Physical Education programmes to lead and engage in collective action strategies that facilitate social pedagogy principles.

VIGNETTE

The Physical Education Teacher Education (PETE) programme faculty at a large university learns that Physical Education teachers in nearby K-12 schools are increasingly expected to participate in school-based professional learning communities (PLCs). Part of the learning community tasks include collectively identifying student learning outcomes, designing common assessments, and establishing curricular decisions based on student data, interests, and cultural norms. There is a problem: many Physical Education teachers express concern with this collaborative approach, having never experienced it as a student in their teacher preparation training with minimal guidance on managing the collective tasks. Recognising the training gap, members of the PETE programme examine and revise existing coursework and fieldwork assignments to resemble the collaborative realities in schools and communities and better prepare preservice Physical Education teachers to engage as members of PLCs. In response, the PETE programme faculty places preservice teachers in meaningful groups called "communities" and embeds group problem-solving as a signature feature to promote learning within the

DOI: 10.4324/9781003411536-7

programme. Furthermore, the PETE faculty regularly meet with the local teachers and attend the PLC meetings at schools to stay abreast of the current trends and school-level issues impacting teachers. The PETE programme creates a new course focused on policy and social promotion advocacy to assist preservice teachers in working collaboratively with administrators, school boards, colleagues, and community agencies to produce equitable and meaningful change for the students they serve.

Introduction

Efforts to innovate and reform Physical Education have often taken a singular approach, focusing on isolated and specialised tasks (Ward et al., 2021). Unfortunately, these solo ventures have not led to significant overall improvement. This is partially due to the unique position of Physical Education being at the intersection of three major social and socialising forces: public health, sport, and education (Lawson, 2020). While this intersection has some advantages, it also presents inherent challenges. The different groups and professional organisations within these domains need help with competing goals and priorities regarding the purpose, objectives, and outcomes of K-12 Physical Education.

Moreover, complex social constructs such as health disparities, racial injustice, poverty, food insecurity, and limited access to essential health services have a significant impact on population-based health and well-being. These factors consequently hinder students' readiness to learn and diminish the potential effects of school-based Physical Education on health. It's important to note that these issues are not confined to the North American context alone. The World Health Organization recognises the influence of societal factors on children's health, stating that "the circumstances of [children and youths] are shaped by the distribution of money, power, and resources at global, national, and local levels, which is mostly responsible for health inequities" (WHO, n.d.).

Lawson (2020) advocates that school-based Physical Education should move beyond a narrow focus on medicalised health. He states, "Human well-being and social welfare are lost in the dominant view of health determinants" (p. 81). Expanding the outcomes of Physical Education beyond a medical model aligns with the principles of social pedagogy as the holistic needs of the child and the promotion of human welfare are prioritised. Yet, in addressing the complex social factors that impact child health and welfare, collaboration among specialised professionals across schools, community agencies, health care settings, and social services is crucial. If we adopt a systems perspective, Physical Education can be viewed and reconceptualised more comprehensively, and the interplay of social determinants can be acknowledged, which influences the overall well-being of children and youth

(Lawson, 2020). Coordinated efforts among different settings and specialised professionals have the potential to systematically enhance the mental, emotional, and physical well-being of children and youth.

A system comprises interconnected elements organised to achieve a specific purpose (Stroh, 2015). Systems frameworks draw attention to the relationships among components and provide insights into how the components influence one another. In Physical Education, pursuing the ideal one best system may crowd out critical pedagogical approaches or models that embrace a human-centred perspective. That is why societal changes and advancements in the 21st century call for a new and diversified approach that embraces the human-centred perspective of social pedagogy in adopting a systems perspective.

Physical Education as a Social System

Framed by systems thinking, Physical Education not only interacts with and overlaps societal sectors (e.g., social work, sport, recreation, education, public health), it is, itself, a system comprising several core components (e.g., school programmes, teacher education, doctoral education, policy, professional associations) that influence and are influenced by one another (Lawson, 2020). Physical Education as a social system is critical for at least two reasons. First, it provides a framework for understanding how one component associated with Physical Education influences and is influenced by others. For example, innovation and improvement in Physical Education Teacher Education (PETE) has the potential to impact K-12 schoolteachers, programmes, and students. Likewise, national and local policies influence PETE and school programmes. Second, critical analyses of component relationships can pinpoint effective and sub-optimal practices that are ignored or left undiscovered and unresolved. When relationships among components are examined, they can reveal the (in)efficiencies, identify perceived vs. actual outcomes, and assist leaders in determining "what is" while accelerating transformative action towards "what should be". For example, national organisations may identify essential standards and grade-level outcomes. However, research may suggest that many teachers do not teach to these standards. Likewise, supportive national or local policy initiatives may be in place limiting the number of students to 40 per class. Yet, many schools still assign 60-70 students to a single Physical Education class and teacher. College and university programmes may discover that the instructional models and methodologies taught to preservice teachers do not align with teaching practices at local K-12 schools.

As an important reminder, the conceptualization of Physical Education as a social system promotes unity and invites collective action. This should not be misunderstood as a suggestion of conformity or *sameness*. Unity is shaped by a common agenda targeting social change and equity, but it is also based on justifiable (e.g., evidence-based, theoretically driven) diversity and malleability (Ward et al., 2021). This means that guiding, moral principles influence practice, but the application of those principles remains nimble and responsive to variables unique to local contexts and needs.

Mindful of the system-level complexities, collective action must follow suit. Systems require teamwork and shared experience to address broader social issues related to the profession. Collective action has been defined as "an approach where multiple parties work together, taking tangible steps through planning and labour, to reach a common goal based on a timely, important agenda" (Beddoes & Jones, 2022, p. 253). Collective action compels boundary-crossing and bridge-building to address 21st-century challenges like improving or (re)designing suboptimal K-12 programmes, establishing cross-sector partnerships, designing for context- and learner-specific needs, and increasing outcomes accountability measures for programmes and professionals (Beddoes & Jones, 2022; Jones et al., 2023). The need for collective action aligns with social pedagogy principles, which identify individual members of the system as inherently resourceful, mindful of their setting, empowered to interact with others and assets within their environment effectively, endowed with agency and capable of influencing positive social change. Moreover, collective action appeals to **The Common Third** as shared activities bring people and perspectives together in a non-hierarchical fashion.

Lawson and colleagues (2021) highlighted important aspects of collective action. Collective action formations can be organised within three spheres of influence – personal, organisational, and cross-sector. Some notable examples include *inter*school and *intra*school professional learning communities ([PLCs]; Beddoes et al., 2019), networked improvement communities) Bryk et al., 2015) and school, family, and community partnerships (Lewallen et al., 2015). PLCs can provide place-based, teacher/student-centred processes to mobilise efforts, action, and outcomes around teacher improvement and student learning. They can also be used for collective advocacy purposes at the local level. Organised together, teams of teachers have been observed creating a critical mass necessary for social promotion and producing notable changes in local policy (Beddoes et al., 2021). As stated at the beginning of this charter (see vignette), many Physical Education teachers express concern with this collaborative approach, having never experienced it as a student in their teacher preparation studies.

Networked improvement communities can be valuable collective action formations for members of entire organisations, such as whole schools or district-wide efforts (Bryk et al., 2015), to learn together, conduct action research, and engage in improvement sharing. An illustrative example of school, family, and community partnerships is the Whole School, Whole

Community, Whole Child ([WSCC]; Lewallen et al., 2015) approach. The WSCC highlights the interdependent nature of policies, practices, and procedures aimed at nurturing the comprehensive development of learners. This approach emphasises purposeful, planned, and meaningful interactions across various aspects of a school system, including nutrition services, health education, the physical environment, health services, counselling, psychological and social services, Physical Education, employee wellness, and community involvement. By bringing together education leaders and health professionals who frequently work in the same setting and serve the same children, the WSCC model promotes collaboration that better addresses the holistic needs of those they support. To achieve a common objective, coordinated efforts among education and health professionals within the school and with relevant community connections are vital (e.g., social and emotional learning is embedded into the school curricula across every subject and grade level, including Physical Education). The WSCC framework emphasises collective endeavours to enhance children's cognitive, physical, social, and emotional development, incorporating numerous interrelated social components such as community involvement, family engagement, the social and emotional climate, Physical Education, physical activity, and social services. The WSCC model is an actionable framework for organised collective action (Lewallen et al., 2015).

Collective action models, like the WSCC framework, may be particularly suitable for advancing social pedagogy in Physical Education because they (a) guide for addressing social issues within an educational framework, (b) prioritise a reflexive relationship with community needs and services beyond the school, and (c) conceptualise student well-being as multi-dimensional, requiring multi-component approaches. In essence, no single group of professionals or individuals located in schools or communities are positioned alone to effectively handle children's intricate and ever-changing social, emotional, and physical needs. Instead, it is crucial to establish collective action formations that embrace evidence-based approaches to leverage their peers' strengths, expertise, and specialised knowledge within a shared space, all working towards the goal of promoting the well-being and success of children.

Collective Action Imperatives for the Physical Education Workforce System

Making collective action a top priority within the Physical Education system may necessitate a paradigm shift. The effectiveness of collective action hinges on its prioritisation among various stakeholders in the Physical Education workforce, including teachers, prospective teachers, teacher educators, and policy actors (Jones et al., 2023). With adequate training to foster collaboration within and across different components, the Physical Education system will enact its potential and achieving meaningful change on a larger scale will be feasible.

The guiding principles of social pedagogy, which emphasise dialogue and teamwork, necessitate cross-sector collaboration within an environment of mutual respect (participation). While this statement may seem straightforward, its actual implementation relies on successfully navigating traditional and intricate role expectations, responsibilities, and cultural challenges. To illustrate this, we will examine cultural challenges within both PETE and school Physical Education programmes. By focusing on these two components from a systems perspective, we aim to highlight potential avenues for strengthening their relationship, facilitating other forms of intercomponent and cross-sector collective action and reflection.

Physical Education Teacher Education

PETE programmes are responsible for equipping preservice teachers with specialised skills, knowledge, and dispositions while challenging existing notions about the purpose and benefits of Physical Education for children and youth today. Ideally, PETE programmes should be positioned to question the status quo and advocate for social transformations when necessary. As preservice teachers navigate their preparation journey, they are influenced by professors, peers, classroom and clinical experiences, and other formal and informal experiences. Pedagogical practices associated with behaviour management, planning, instruction, assessment, and content knowledge play a significant role in their socialisation process. However, important aspects such as collaboration, relationship building, collective action, bridge-building, student empowerment, social and emotional learning, and addressing the needs of the whole child may need more attention in many PETE programmes.

From a systems perspective, fostering collaborative principles in higher education is easier said than done. Academic culture often clashes with the concepts of collective action because of the need for togetherness combined with implicit and explicit power hierarchies. Department members and faculty within the same programme may hold differing philosophies and choose to work independently, potentially working at cross-purposes. Furthermore, college and university incentive structures typically do not prioritise or reward collaborative efforts that extend beyond scholarly output. These dynamics must be considered when striving for social pedagogic change, innovation, or improvement within and for the Physical Education system.

School Physical Education

The challenges to collective action within PETE programmes discussed above also extend to K-12 school programmes, as aspiring Physical Education teachers have historically been socialised to work in isolation (Lortie, 1975). In other words, teachers need to learn how to engage collaboratively within a culture of togetherness because novice Physical Education teachers enter a school with an established culture that may or may not prioritise collaboration. Work-role conflicts, such as the tensions between coaching and teaching, unclear expectations, and marginalisation, can further limit their motivation and capacity to engage in collective action (Richards et al., 2014). If the circumstances take place, teachers may continue to operate in isolation and perhaps leave many of their students' needs unmet.

To avoid the above circumstances, fostering connections between preservice physical educators, social workers, school nurses or healthcare providers, education administrators, and professionals in public health, business, engineering, economics, and more holds potential for future collective action. Such collaborations can pioneer strategies within schools (e.g., one such strategy is mentioned in the vignette at the beginning of this chapter as group problem-solving that is used as a signature feature to promote learning) to enhance social consciousness and support youth and child development. With this understanding, let's explore examples of how collective action can be pursued within the Physical Education system.

Preparing Preservice Physical Education Teachers for Collective Action towards Social Pedagogy

PETE programmes hold the potential to be genuinely team-oriented (e.g., people working towards a common goal; Salas et al., 2015). This includes thinking beyond programmes and departments to include cross-sector collaboration. For example, though not necessarily programme-specific, PETE faculty could serve on an advisory board which includes exercise physiologists, experts in strength and conditioning, physical therapists, dietitians, social and mental health experts, and communications directors, which serves to monitor and strengthen youth sport programmes. Additionally, PETE faculty could draw upon the expertise of social workers and psychologists via invitations as guest speakers in preparation courses.

Teamwork requires combining at least two essential elements: structures and team dynamics (Beddoes et al., 2023). Structures imply a designated system for collaboration (e.g., regular, organised meeting times). Team dynamics encompass the attitudes, behaviours, and cognitions (thinking patterns aligned with **The Common Third**) that shape the team's culture. Like school-based PLCs, PETE faculty within the same programme must be cautious to avoid allowing philosophical differences to erode trust, communication, and collaboration. It is essential to allow colleagues to retain personal academic freedom in adapting teaching styles according to their unique needs and personalities while also maintaining respect and compromise where unity of purpose safeguards the development of students over individual interests. To be skilful and respectful collaborators, preservice teachers must witness this process repeatedly and openly among the professors who guide them (Beddoes & Jones, 2022).

Fostering Physical Education Preservice Teacher Growth in Relationship Building and Collaboration

Preservice teachers must learn by intentionally engaging with others to foster the collaborative skills necessary to become social change agents. It cannot be assumed that preservice teachers will automatically adopt a disposition towards collective action or cross-discipline collaboration by observation alone. Like other forms of knowledge and behaviours, collective action requires a skillset that must be explicitly taught (Dillard, 2016).

Given that collective action takes intentional and proactive effort, PETE programmes may better serve their students by engaging them in frequent and progressive opportunities to solve problems, establish group norms within a culture of mutual respect and examine issues from various perspectives and specialised lenses. For example, early PETE programme courses could encourage group work and problem-solving around a particular problem of practice. These activities could help prepare preservice teachers for participation (active listening, reflecting on assumptions, preparing for interactions with others, and making decisions).

Advanced methods courses could be designed as class-level PLCs where preservice teachers engage in clinical experiences, design learning objectives, align assessments, and analyse student-level performance data in small group settings. Preservice teachers completing their student teaching may be required to participate in a school-level PLC or other collective action formation at the school, district, or community levels. PETE faculty could likewise include preservice teachers in collaborative problem-solving exercises or volunteering for community-led physical activity, recreational programmes, social service agencies, or health care settings.

Empowering in-Service Teachers for Local Collective Action

Many schools are reflecting the global workforce trend towards interdependence and collaboration. As student learning and emotional needs grow increasingly complex, collective action in education is a contemporary imperative. According to Hord and Sommers (2008), collective action within PLCs may include (a) shared and supportive leadership, (b) shared values, visions, and goals, (c) collective learning and application, (d) shared individual practice, and (e) supportive conditions. Aligned with social pedagogy, a PLC can engender well-being and empowerment by fostering collective curiosity around a common issue, promoting individual responsibility, and creating a safe space of trust to share important information. Moreover, a PLC may provide a supportive framework for operationalising **The Three Ps**: (a) *professional*, e.g., evidence-based practice, theory, and research opportunities; (b) *personal* e.g., reciprocity cultivated through relationship building; and (c) *private*, e.g., all collaboration efforts benefit each participating teacher and every student.

In a global society, social media and other digital platforms can be helpful tools for idea-sharing and help-seeking (Ferreira et al., 2022). That said, we advocate for teachers to form and/or contribute to school-based, local communities of like-minded professionals that encompass the PLC defining characteristics. PLCs can be structured to provide a systematised response to student learning and intervention (DuFour & Eaker, 1998) and for localised groups of teachers they can be set up to organise for collective action and advocacy (Beddoes et al., 2021). The opening vignette to this chapter demonstrates the interrelationship of the Physical Education system components, PETE, and school Physical Education programmes. As schools become increasingly collaborative, PETE must prepare professionals to engage in PLC-like collective action formations. Further, PETE should prioritise engagement and relationship-building with local schools and teachers. Collective action invites the collaborative engagement of all who influence young people within the Physical Education system.

Key Points

- Physical Education encompasses a system with interdependent and interrelated components.
- Collective action within and between Physical Education system components is essential.
- PETE programmes should prepare Physical Education teacher graduates to utilise collective action formations like professional learning communities.
- Physical Education teachers can foster student learning and collective action via professional learning communities.

Advice from the Field

My name is Tara Hall. I am in my 16th year of teaching high school Physical Education. I have coached varsity girls' basketball and have taught Physical Education subjects that include weight training, body conditioning, individual lifetime activities, participation skills and techniques, and fitness for life, as well as secondary health II classes and Sports Medicine in the classroom. For the past year, I have been serving as the district-wide PLC representative for physical educators. I lead a team of 10 district Physical Education professionals who work with school PLC teams to development common curricula, align formative assessment tools with essential learning outcomes, and deliver learning experiences based on those data. In this role, I serve as a liaison among the district administrators, schools, Physical Education teachers, and local PETE faculty members. Our goal is to represent collective action and work together through nested and supported teams to meet the needs of our students. In my role as a director of a district-wide PLC team, I have learned that relationships are an important first step. I have learned to be patient with myself and others and need to constantly remind myself that establishing a functioning PLC team will take time and energy. Most importantly we are seeking to change culture, especially when it comes to Physical Education teachers who are often highly confident and/or comfortable in much of what they are currently doing. Change sometimes means discomfort. Collaborating sometimes brings out vulnerability in people. All these elements of the process need to be treated with care so that relationships of trust and camaraderie can be built to encourage effective collaboration and teamwork as the process moves forward into more productive work related to student-learning outcomes. When team members have positive relationships of trust and respect, I think this can be a motivator to begin working together. Finally, I've learned through my own experience as an adult-learner and member of a collaborative team that adults need to take responsibility for their own personal and professional development; usually they don't appreciate being told what to do or how to do it. This is especially true if they don't feel any ownership or buy-in to the collective work! Choice is important. Purpose is important. Validation is important! Give everyone the opportunity to choose what important role they can commit to in the collective work and establish norms that will encourage them to carry out their role. Then, take time to CELEBRATE together when everyone is fulfilling their roles and helping the collective work more forward. Celebrating everyone's strengths builds teamwork and both individual and group efficacy.

Reflection Questions and Activities

1 How does systems thinking and collective action within Physical Education forward social pedagogy concepts?
2 How can PETE programmes and K-12 teachers collectively advance principles of social pedagogy?

References

Beddoes, Z., & Jones, E. (2022). Enhancing collective action in Physical Education teacher education: A three-pathways approach. *Quest, 74*(3), 251–265. https://doi.org/10.1080/00336297.2022.2085590

Beddoes, Z., Prusak, K., Beighle, A., & Pennington, T. (2021). Utilizing school-based, professional learning communities to enhance Physical Education programs and facilitate systems change (Part 2). *Quest, 73*(3), 294-305. https://doi.org/10.1080/00336297.2021.1915351

Beddoes, Z., Prusak, K., Barney, D., & Pennington, T. (2023). Attending to the emotional side of professional learning communities (PLCs) by cultivating positive team dynamics. *Journal of Physical Education, Recreation & Dance, 94*(4), 21–25. https://doi.org/10.1080/07303084.2023.2172114

Bryk, A.S., Gomez, L.M., Grunow, A., & LeMahieu, P.G. (2015). *Learning to improve: How America's schools can get better at getting better.* Harvard Education Press.

Dillard, H.K. (2016). Pre-service training in professional learning communities benefits novice teacher. *Transformative Dialogues: Teaching and Learning Journal, 9*(2), 1–3. Retrieved from https://journals.psu.edu/td/article/view/1045.

DuFour, R., & Eaker, R. (1998). *Professional learning communities.* National Educational Service.

Ferreira, H.J., Gonçalves, L., & Parker, M. (2022). Physical Education teachers' experiences of nurturing a community of practice online. *Journal of Teaching in Physical Education, 1*(aop), 1–10. https://doi.org/10.1123/jtpe.2021-0305

Hord, S.M., & Sommers, W.A. (Eds.). (2008). *Leading professional learning communities: Voices from research and practice.* Corwin Press.

Jones, E.M., Lawson, H.A., & Richards, K.A. (2023). Operationalizing a Physical Education workforce research and development agenda. *Quest, 74*(4), 374–388. https://doi.org/10.1080/00336297.2022.2142916

Lawson, H.A. (2020). The Physical Education system as a consequential social determinant. *Quest, 72*(1), 72–84. https://doi.org/10.1080/00336297.2019.1627224

Lawson, H.A., Jones, E., Beddoes, Z., Estes, S., Morris, S.A., Mitchell, M.F., ... & Ward, P. (2021). Collective action for learning, improvement, and redesign. *Journal of Teaching in Physical Education, 40*(3), 412–422. https://doi.org/10.1123/jtpe.2020-0246

Lewallen, T.C., Hunt, H., Potts-Datema, W., Zaza, S., & Giles, W. (2015). The whole school, whole community, whole child model: A new approach for improving educational attainment and healthy development for students. *Journal of School Health, 85*(11), 729–739. https://doi.org/10.1111/josh.12310

Lortie, D. (1975). *Schoolteacher. A sociological study.* University of Chicago Press.

Richards, K.A.R., Templin, T.J., & Graber, K. (2014). The socialization of teachers in Physical Education: Review and recommendations for future works. *Kinesiology Review, 3*(2), 113–134. https://doi.org/10.1123/kr.2013-0006

Salas, E., Shuffler, M.L., Thayer, A.L., Bedwell, W.L., & Lazzara, E.H. (2015). Understanding and improving teamwork in organizations: A scientifically based practical guide. *Human Resource Management, 54*(4), 599–622. https://doi.org/10.1002/hrm.21628

Stroh, D.P. (2015). *Systems thinking for social change: A practical guide to solving complex problems, avoiding unintended consequences, and achieving lasting results.* Chelsea Green Publishing.

Ward, P., Lawson, H.A., van der Mars, H., & Mitchell, M.F. (2021). 21st century Physical Education in the United States: Introduction to the special issue. *Journal of Teaching in Physical Education, 40*(3), 345–352. https://doi.org/10.1123/jtpe.2020-0239

Word Health Organization [WHO]. (n.d.). Social determinants of health. https://www.who.int/social_determinants/sdh_definition/en/

5 Strategies for Enacting Social Pedagogy in Physical Education

Alan Ovens and Hannah Stow

Learning Objectives

At the end of this chapter, you will be able to:
- Understand how the principles of social pedagogy can guide the strategies you use in Physical Education.
- Know and apply five strategies to enact social pedagogy in Physical Education.
- Appreciate the need to adapt and modify strategies to suit the students in each lesson context.

VIGNETTE

John felt a mix of excitement and curiosity as he walked into his Physical Education class. He always enjoyed the lessons with Ms Lopez, his teacher, because she liked to co-create each unit with the students. They had agreed to choreograph a dance routine incorporating different cultural dance traditions for the dance unit they were doing now. This involved the class dividing into different groups, with some members of the class acting as choreographers designing the routine, while others acting as teachers working with small groups of different abilities and interests. John wasn't a confident dancer, so as part of his learning plan, he chose to be part of a group of beginner dancers learning about hip-hop from Jenny, who was a good dancer. Their moves would be incorporated into the whole class routine later in the unit. Ms. Lopez monitored what was happening throughout the lesson and only interacted with people when needed. At the end of the lesson, the class gathered in a circle to discuss the lesson and provide feedback on things that could be improved next time. John shared how he was starting to feel more confident and acknowledged Jenny for her excellent leadership of the group. As he left the lesson, he noted the moves he would have to practice.

DOI: 10.4324/9781003411536-8

Introduction

This chapter outlines key strategies and practical examples to guide teachers towards implementing social pedagogy in Physical Education. The aim is to think about how teachers can create an environment that encourages and supports positive relationships, promotes respect for cultural diversity and inclusion, and provides opportunities for personal development towards independence, but also has a socialising function in reinforcing social solidarity and interdependence (Eichsteller & Holthoff, 2012). We start by outlining what we mean by strategy and suggest that being an adaptive, reflective professional is core to effectively implementing the strategies. We then outline five strategies that we think are good starting points for anyone interested in exploring how to implement a social pedagogy in their own programme.

In the realm of social pedagogy, teaching strategies play a vital role in creating effective learning environments. We define a teaching strategy as a deliberate approach teachers use to facilitate learning, engage students, and achieve desired educational outcomes. Strategies encompass a range of instructional methods, techniques, and tactics designed to organise and structure educational experiences, ensuring that these are purposeful, coherent, and effective. In social pedagogy, effective teaching strategies are characterised by their ability to create a sense of belonging for all learners, foster student interaction, encourage critical thinking and creativity, build a community of learners, and shape Physical Education to be more responsive and meaningful to students' aspirations (Jelly et al., 2013; Roberts & Bolstad, 2010).

However, it is important to recognise that strategies are not prescriptive techniques that should be followed like a recipe. Rather, they represent potential ways of organising the lesson that aligns with and bring to life the teacher's fundamental values and beliefs (Black et al., 2015). The ability to successfully use a strategy, particularly concerning social pedagogy, greatly depends on several factors. First, it requires a shift from a teacher-centred approach to a learning-centred approach. This involves engaging in meaningful conversations with students, trusting their capabilities, and using 'student voice to develop learner agency, as the students help to identify and address issues in their learning environments' (Timperley et al., 2014, p. 6). Second, it requires adaptive expertise to blend strategies in response to the specific situation of each teacher's context. Adaptive expertise (Timperley, 2022) is characterised by innovation and flexibility as the teacher navigates the complexities of the classroom environment, adapting the strategies and orchestrating the lesson in relation to the unique strengths, challenges, and interests of their students and the novel situations that arise. Third, it requires an ongoing commitment to enquiry, reflection, and growth. While the principles of social pedagogy provide a foundation, the teacher should also constantly reflect on their practice and make informed decisions to ensure the strategies are effectively implemented (Cameron et al., 2011).

Strategies for Enacting Social Pedagogy in Physical Education 63

At the opening vignette in this chapter, students would co-create a dance routine incorporating different cultural dance traditions for their dance unit. This would mean that Mrs Lopez would have to adapt her strategies based on how the lesson would unfold.

In the following section, we focus on five specific strategies embodying the principles and values of social pedagogy. These strategies offer practical guidance for teachers seeking to enact a social pedagogical approach in their classrooms. By implementing these strategies, teachers can create an inclusive and empowering learning environment that nurtures student agency, holistic development, and meaningful engagement.

Students as Co-contributors to Programme and Unit Design

Inviting students as co-contributors to the design of programmes and units of work is an inclusive strategy based on the belief that students have a right and a responsibility to be involved in decisions related to their learning. It is based on the social pedagogy principle that teachers *work with* instead *work for* students (see Chapter 2). This strategy recognises students' inherent worth and agency and acknowledges their insights, experiences, and perspectives. By involving students in the key decisions around course design, teachers foster a collaborative and inclusive learning environment that becomes more meaningful and responsive to students' interests and aspirations (Howley & Tannehill, 2014). It helps build a sense of co-ownership, trust, belonging and community within the classroom (Enright & O'Sullivan, 2010), facilitating teacher-student and student-student relationships and increasing the meaningfulness of Physical Education for students.

As a strategy, inviting students to become co-contributors to their courses can take various forms, such as surveying students and parents, gathering feedback from student representatives, and employing exit tickets at the end of lessons. One method we have found very powerful is to create a *Student Course Committee* from members of the class who are either elected or volunteer to be part of the committee. The committee's role is representing the class, meeting with the teacher throughout the course, and contributing to the course design. Regardless of the method chosen, the aim is to be inclusive and foster meaningful discussions that guide the course design process. Such discussions could happen throughout the course and can indicatively focus on aspects shown in Table 5.1.

By encouraging students to voice their preferences and obstacles in the learning process, teachers can create a more meaningful, relevant, and engaging course. Ultimately, this approach emphasises the value of student agency and promotes a vibrant learning community where students feel empowered to participate actively and contribute to their own educational experiences.

Table 5.1 The Student Course Committee strategy

Prior to the course beginning, discuss with students:	a What content and outcomes would be most meaningful and relevant for their learning. b What forms of teaching supports their learning best. c What methods could be used to demonstrate and assess their learning.
During the course, gather feedback on:	a What's going well and what needs to be revised. b Whether student needs are being met
After the course has concluded, encourage students to:	a Evaluate all aspects of the teaching, including the content and outcomes, learning activities, and forms of assessment. b Write a report and recommendation for next year's course committee

Negotiated Learning and Assessment Plans

Another strategy based on the principle of *working with* students is supporting them in developing and negotiating their learning and assessment plans. The important concept here is that these plans are 'negotiated' with students rather than allowing students to choose what happens in each lesson. The aim is to encourage students to think about their learning needs and consider how assessment can best support their learning journey. This strategy not only empowers students to engage with their learning progress actively but also allows them to set personal goals, co-create learning activities and assessment criteria, and reflect on their growth. It paves the way for a more equitable and student-driven approach by relinquishing the traditional hierarchy between teacher and student.

Various studies in Physical Education support the use of negotiated learning and assessment plans, suggesting that allowing students to co-construct the learning environment afforded them a sense of control, confidence, and connection with the aims of Physical Education. For example, working with students to negotiate their learning plans has been shown to aid in addressing self-identified barriers to physical activity and increasing physical activity opportunities (Oliver et al, 2009). It can also aid in helping students to think constructively about their own Physical Education, connect with the Physical Education curriculum, and find the subject more meaningful (Guadalupe & Curtner-Smith, 2020). However, negotiating learning plans is challenging, and students and teachers must persevere beyond the initial novelty and change the status quo (Enright & O'Sullivan, 2010).

Negotiating an individual learning and assessment plan with a student involves a collaborative and communicative process (Table 5.2). Here are the steps a teacher might follow:

Strategies for Enacting Social Pedagogy in Physical Education 65

Table 5.2 Negotiating an individual learning and assessment plan with a student

Initiate the Conversation	Begin by initiating a conversation with the student. Express the intention to collaboratively design a learning and assessment plan to better cater to their individual needs, interests and learning style.
Identify Learning Goals	Work with the student to identify their learning goals. Discuss both short-term and long-term objectives. This step involves understanding the student's aspirations, challenges, and preferences in the learning process
Assessment Preferences	Discuss the student's preferred methods of assessment. Some students might excel in certain types of assessments (e.g., projects, presentations, written exams), while others may struggle. Tailor the assessment methods to align with the student's strengths and preferences.
Develop a Timeline	Establish a timeline for achieving the identified learning goals. Break down larger goals into smaller, manageable steps with achievable milestones. This provides a clear roadmap for both the student and the teacher.
Regular Check-Ins	Schedule regular check-ins to assess progress, address concerns, and make any necessary adjustments to the plan. Regular communication helps maintain a collaborative and supportive learning environment.
Document the Plan	Document the individual learning and assessment plan in writing. This formalises the agreement and serves as a reference for both the teacher and the student. Include details such as learning goals, assessment methods, accommodations, and the agreed-upon timeline.
Celebrate Achievements	Recognise and celebrate the student's achievements as they progress through the plan. Positive reinforcement contributes to motivation and reinforces the value of the collaborative learning process.

This strategy places assessment at the nexus of democratic participation and reflective learning within Physical Education. Involving students in the assessment process empowers them to take ownership of their learning outcomes and encourages their critical thinking, metacognition, and a heightened sense of accountability.

Culturally Responsive Teaching

The social pedagogy principle that interpersonal relationships are mediators of teaching and learning underpins the strategy of culturally responsive teaching. At its core, this strategy seeks to create an inclusive and affirming learning environment where all students' identities, cultures, characteristics, languages, and perspectives are respected and integrated into the educational process (Morrison et al., 2019). Many scholars are concerned that students from indigenous and marginalised backgrounds are disadvantaged and underperforming in schools. This is often because their culture and experiences are not considered integral to who they are as learners or how they make sense of the world. In contrast, the strategy of culturally responsive teaching relates to the idea that all students should be able to see themselves, their identities and their cultures reflected through the curriculum, lesson activities and classroom interactions. As Gay (2002, p. 106) notes, 'When academic knowledge and skills are situated within the lived experiences and frames of reference for students, they are more personally meaningful, have higher interest appeal, and are learned more easily and thoroughly'.

As a strategy for Physical Education, Wrench and Garrett (2021) stress the need to embrace the notion that everything in a lesson interacts as part of a learning eco-system that produces ways of knowing, doing, and being. Rather than simply being a process of placing 'cultural content' into each lesson, culturally responsive teaching shifts attention to the relational aspects of co-creating and shaping meanings around different perspectives and cultures the students bring to each lesson. This includes teachers cultivating awareness of the day-to-day cultural landscapes of their students' lives (Robinson et al., 2013) and designing learning environments and experiences that recognise and value the cultural resources of young people and their families (Flory & McCaughtry, 2011; Young & Sternod, 2011). While there are many ways of doing this, we suggest it is helpful to consider this strategy having three key components:

- **Challenging the deficit thinking** that is often used to explain continued educational disparities and behavioural issues (Bishop, 2019). As discussed in Chapter 1, deficit thinking refers to a negative and often biased perspective that focuses on students' perceived weaknesses, limitations, or shortcomings, particularly those from marginalised or underrepresented backgrounds (Valencia, 2010). Deficit thinking manifests in various ways, such as assuming that students from disadvantaged backgrounds are less capable of academic success, attributing their challenges solely to their backgrounds rather than considering systemic factors or using deficit-based language to describe students' abilities or behaviours. It can contribute to educational disparities and hinder efforts to create inclusive and equitable learning environments. In contrast, culturally responsive teaching challenges this mindset by actively countering negative stereotypes and recognising the unique assets, strengths, and funds of knowledge that each student brings to the classroom. It reframes the narrative from deficiency to abundance, acknowledging that students from all backgrounds have valuable cultural, linguistic, and experiential assets that can enrich the learning environment (Jackson, 2011).

- **Employing a "relationships first" approach** in which building strong, empathetic, nurturing relationships is the priority. Teachers who foster caring and learning relationships within their lessons, particularly with indigenous, marginalised and minority students, interact with them in ways that allow them to see themselves as successful learners. It also promotes responsiveness from teachers having a better understanding of students and higher expectations for their learning (Patey et al., 2023). As Bishop (2019) outlines, the objective is to create a family-like environment for learning that is culturally responsive and allows teachers to interact dialogically with learners to promote learning and enhance educational outcomes. These relationships create a safe, supportive space where students feel valued, seen, and heard. In such an environment, students are more likely to engage in meaningful learning, take risks, and develop a sense of belonging. Culturally responsive teaching recognises that when students feel connected to their educators and peers, they are better equipped to navigate the educational journey and achieve their full potential.
- **Seeing students' differences is a valuable resource** that supports learning and enhances the curriculum. A culturally responsive learning environment integrates students' identities, languages, and perspectives into the educational process. It acknowledges the diversity within the classroom and actively seeks to honour and celebrate this diversity. This involves incorporating students' cultural backgrounds, languages, and experiences into the curriculum, instructional materials, and classroom activities. By doing so, culturally responsive teaching ensures that students' identities are respected and integrated into the learning experience, fostering a sense of pride in one's cultural heritage, developing understanding and awareness of different cultures, and a deeper engagement with the content of all students.

As shown in Table 5.3, a culturally responsive teaching strategy includes a variety of actions that teachers could enact.

By acknowledging and valuing our students' diverse backgrounds, experiences, and identities, we lay the foundation for meaningful connections and mutual respect. Culturally responsive teaching prompts us to integrate culturally relevant content, perspectives, and practices into our pedagogical approach. Through this strategy, we bridge the gap between the Physical Education curriculum and the lived realities of our students, fostering a sense of belonging and empowerment.

Incorporating Collaborative Games and Activities

Collaborative games and activities provide opportunities for students to develop positive personal, social, and cultural outcomes central to helping them grow in life, know their strengths, and contribute to others (Ovens et al.,

Table 5.3 Example of a culturally responsive teaching strategy

Reflect on your teaching assumptions related to culture	Evaluate your beliefs about the culturally diverse learners in your classes and consider how your assumptions influence the curriculum decisions and interactions you have with students. Are you willing to go beyond the established and familiar practices to find ways that may be more inclusive, meaningful, and rich for all students?
Learn about your students	Find ways to learn about your students as individuals rather than cultural stereotypes. You could initiate conversations or ask them to write about themselves and their family traditions, or perhaps have them complete a personal questionnaire about their interests, backgrounds, and aspirations. The key is to know your students so you can better engage their frames of reference, life experiences, and cultural values as a basis for building meaningful learning.
Create an inclusive and supportive learning environment based on strong relationships	Care for and nurture every student, communicating high expectations for their learning. Acknowledge them as culturally located individuals and value their language and culture
Use students' cultural knowledge, perspectives, and skills as a resource for teaching	Draw on the students' funds of knowledge so that each lesson facilitates the sharing, appreciation, and integration of students' knowledge, experiences, concerns, questions, and sense-making processes.
Connect with families and communities	Extend your programme into and draw from the wider community. Engage with families and the community regularly and in different ways to help you adapt your teaching for diverse students.

2020). This strategy embodies the social pedagogy principle that interpersonal relationships mediate teaching and learning. By prioritising relationships and fostering student-centred learning, this strategy extends beyond the mere organisation of games and activities to seek and create opportunities that encourage students to engage with one another. Through such interaction, students establish connections and foster deeper bonds by discovering common interests, engaging in conversations, learning collaboratively, sharing experiences, and uncovering facets about themselves and their peers, classmates, and teachers (Baker et al., 2023). In essence, collaborative games and activities are the nucleus of social pedagogy, catalysing its central aims, objectives, and values into tangible practice.

The critical tension here for any teacher introducing collaborative games and activities is ensuring that students collaborate in a way that fosters a social pedagogy perspective. For instance, most games require collaboration to play effectively, but the focus of learning is typically on the techniques and physical skills required. The subtle shift in this strategy is to move the focus of learning to personal and social skills. In other words, the emphasis moves from learning to play the game to using the game to learn about participating, involvement, collaboration, and teamwork. These things are often pushed into the background with the assumption that students will learn to collaborate as they play. However, in this strategy, we suggest they need careful planning, discussion, and facilitation to create game environments that foster and facilitate learning these skills.

Collaborative games are where players work together to achieve a common objective. The goal of a collaborative game is to reduce emphasis on competition and increase emphasis on the social aspects of working in teams and groups. In Table 5.4, we suggest issues which teachers need to emphasise when enacting this strategy.

By embracing collaborative games and activities, we create a microcosm of social interaction, mirroring the values of inclusivity and cooperation underpinning social pedagogy's broader aims. John, the student attending

Table 5.4 Incorporating collaborative games and activities as a social pedagogy strategy

Negotiate and promote the values that underpin collaboration	Begin a unit by encouraging discussion on the key issues that enable and limit collaboration. Seek consensus for important guidelines that facilitate inclusion and participation. This could be achieved through making classroom agreements that are upheld throughout the year, working to 'cultivate a sense of community and belonging and qualities of safety, respect, caring, and even love' (Kochhar-Bryant & Heishman, 2010).
Teach communication skills	Good communication underpins the ability to create a climate of cooperation, positive discipline, and quality learning. Emphasise and teach the skills of good communication, like expressing yourself, active listening, assertiveness, positive interaction, and support. Having good communication skills are core to conflict resolution, enabling students to actively contribute positively to classroom environments, and having the tools to alleviate any adversities when they arise.
Teach about being a productive member of a team or group	If we want to empower students to communicate, cooperate, and contribute constructively within a group setting, we need to teach them about sharing, including others, reducing egocentric play, taking turns, contributing to a common goal, understanding team roles, accepting responsibility, and exploring how best to use the group's strengths to be an effective group. This not only enhances their ability to achieve common goals but also fosters a sense of empathy, adaptability, and leadership that is vital for personal growth and societal well-being.

Mrs Lopez's dance class (see opening vignette) felt more confident after participating in the collaborative dance-making activity. Also, he acknowledged their group's peer leader for their efforts.

Triadic Assessment

Triadic assessment, involving the collaboration of students, teachers, and peers in the assessment process, strongly aligns with the social pedagogy principles of working with students, so that empowerment is attained through the relationships established in a lesson. In a social pedagogical framework, the emphasis is placed on relationships, collaboration, and holistic development. Triadic assessment incorporates these principles by fostering a sense of community within the learning environment. Students, teachers, and peers work together as a cohesive unit, encouraging mutual understanding and shared responsibility for the educational journey (Bores-García et al., 2020). This collaborative approach supports academic development and cultivates interpersonal skills, empathy, and a sense of belonging, all of which are central tenets of social pedagogy.

Furthermore, triadic assessment in social pedagogy empowers students by actively involving them in the evaluation process. By engaging in a dialogue with teachers and peers, students gain valuable insights into their strengths and areas for improvement. This multifaceted feedback loop contributes to a more comprehensive understanding of their own learning processes and encourages a sense of ownership over their educational experiences. The students in this chapter's vignette seemed to find the discussion and feedback at the end of the lesson to be an important and valuable part of their classroom routine. Triadic assessment, focusing on collaboration and shared responsibility, reflects the social pedagogical principle of empowering individuals to actively shape their development within a supportive and collaborative learning community.

Triadic assessment designed to support students in developing self-regulated learning is often conceptualised as a three-phase process: preparation, activity, and reflection. Table 5.5 [adapted from Fletcher (2018)], outlines how this may be done.

In each phase, the teacher is a facilitator, guiding students towards becoming more independent and effective self-regulated learners. The emphasis is on creating a supportive learning environment that nurtures students' abilities to set goals, monitor their progress, and reflect on their learning experiences, aligning with the principles of social pedagogy.

Concluding Thoughts

As we outlined at the start, teaching strategies serve as vital tools in shaping a transformative learning environment to enact a social pedagogy perspective. These deliberate approaches, orchestrated by educators, encompass the techniques used to facilitate learning and the fundamental values and beliefs

Strategies for Enacting Social Pedagogy in Physical Education 71

Table 5.5 The three-phase process of triadic assessment

Preparation phase	In the preparation phase, the teacher's role is to guide students in setting meaningful goals and planning how best to achieve these. Teachers can do this by helping students to: • Clarify their learning goals and intentions. • Explore possible learning activities that will facilitate their learning. • Decide what strategies and milestones they will use to monitor progress. • Determine timelines for milestones and assessment activities.
Action phase	During the activity phase, students engage with the learning activities and use the feedback from formative assessment to guide their learning. Teachers can facilitate this by helping students to: • Monitor their learning by focusing student attention on the feedback from assessment activities. • Interpret the evidence and reflect on its meaning. • Adjust the learning strategies and activities.
Reflection phase	The reflection phase is crucial for reinforcing self-regulated learning behaviours and helping students develop metacognitive awareness. Teachers can support this phase by helping students to: • Identify strengths and areas to improve for next time. • Attribute reasons for success and challenges.

underpinning them. The five teaching strategies outlined in this chapter align with the principles of social pedagogy, fostering a sense of belonging, promoting student interaction, nurturing critical thinking and creativity, and building a vibrant community of learners. Yet, the efficacy of these strategies hinges on the teacher's ability to adapt them to suit the diverse dynamics of their classroom. While the principles of social pedagogy lay the groundwork, the teacher's role as a facilitator brings them to life. This calls for a shift from dictating the learning process to empowering students through learner agency. As teachers navigate this complex landscape, they engage in meaningful dialogue, foster connections, and commit to continuous reflection and growth. By recognising the symbiotic relationship between teaching strategies and the educator's flexibility, transformative educational experiences emerge, echoing the core ethos of social pedagogy.

Advice from the Field

Jason Borland (Pukekohe High School, Auckland, New Zealand):

Social pedagogy is something that really interests me. I work in a school located in a low-income area with a large diversity of ethnicities and cultures. Our biggest challenge is on how to enhance the level of achievement of our students. My greatest frustration is the perception

> that my students can't learn. I draw on many of the strategies and ideas outlined in the chapter to address this perception. I am highly aware of how important it is to develop a programme that is meaningful and relevant to student interests and needs. In this sense, I support the idea of finding ways to have students share in designing our Physical Education curriculum, taking responsibility for their learning, and being culturally and socially competent. At the same time, I also appreciate that dealing with young people, especially when there is a high level of diversity, is challenging. I agree wholeheartedly that, while the strategies outlined are essential, they are not easy to implement. They are not a recipe, but a guide for experimentation and adaption. In my view, social pedagogy should be the core that orients Physical Education. It made me realise the value of social pedagogy in everything that we do.

Reflection Questions and Activities

1 Which of the strategies outlined in this chapter most closely aligns with your own philosophy of teaching?
2 What are the factors that mediate a teacher's ability to successfully use a strategy to implement a social pedagogy in their teaching?
3 How are the principles of a social pedagogy reflected in each of the strategies outlined in this chapter?

References

Black, E., Bettencourt, M., & Cameron, C. (2015). *Social pedagogy in the classroom. Supporting children and young people in care.* Retrieved from https://sppa-uk.org/wp-content/uploads/2017/09/Social-Pedagogy-in-the-Classroom.pdf

Bores-García, D., Hortigüela-Alcalá, D., González-Calvo, G., Barba-Martín, R. (2020). Peer assessment in physical education: A systematic review of the last five years. *Sustainability. 12*(21), 9233. https://doi.org/10.3390/su12219233

Cameron, C., Petrie, P., Wigfall, V., Kleipoedszus, S., & Jasper, A. (2011). *Final report of the social pedagogy pilot programme: Development and implementation.* Retrieved from https://discovery.ucl.ac.uk/id/eprint/1532264

Eichsteller, G., & Holthoff, S. (2012). The art of being a social pedagogue: Developing cultural change in children's homes in Essex. *International Journal of Social Pedagogy, 1*(1), 30–45. https://doi.org/10.14324/111.444.ijsp.2012.v1.1.004

Enright, E., & O'Sullivan, M. (2010). 'Can I do it in my pyjamas?' Negotiating a physical education curriculum with teenage girls. *European Physical Education Review, 16*(3), 203–222. https://doi.org/10.1177/1356336X10382967

Fletcher, A. (2018). Classroom assessment as a reciprocal practice to develop students' agency: A social cognitive perspective. *Assessment Matters, 12*, 34–57. https://doi.org/10.18296/am.0032

Flory, S.B., & McCaughtry, N. (2011). Culturally relevant physical education in urban Schools. *Research Quarterly for Exercise and Sport, 82*(1), 49–60. https://doi.org/10.1080/02701367.2011.10599721

Gay, G. (2002). Preparing for culturally responsive teaching. *Journal of Teacher Education*, 53(2), 106–116. https://doi.org/10.1177/0022487102053002003

Guadalupe, T., & Curtner-Smith, M. (2020). 'It's nice to have choices': Influence of purposefully negotiating the curriculum on the students in one mixed-gender middle school class and their teacher. *Sport, Education and Society*, 25(8), 904–916, https://doi.org/10.1080/13573322.2019.1674275

Howley, D., & Tannehill, D. (2014). "Crazy ideas": Student involvement in negotiating and implementing the physical education curriculum in the Irish senior cycle. *Physical Educator*, 71(3), 391–416.

Jackson, Y. (2011). *The pedagogy of confidence: Inspiring high intellectual performance in urban schools.* Teachers College Press.

Jelly, M., Fuller, A., & Byers, R. (2013). *Involving pupils in practice: Promoting partnerships with pupils with special educational needs.* Routledge.

Kochhar-Bryant, C.A., & Heishman, A. (Eds.). (2010). *Effective collaboration for educating the whole child.* Corwin Press.

Morrison, A., Rigney, L.-I., Hattam, R., & Diplock, A. (2019). *Toward and Australian culturally responsive pedagogy: A narrative review of the literature.* University of South Australia.

Oliver, K.L., Hamzeh, M., & McCaughtry, N. (2009). Girly girls can play games / Las niñas pueden jugar tambien: Co-creating a curriculum of possibilities with fifth-grade girls. *Journal of Teaching in Physical Education*, 28(1), 90–110. https://doi.org/10.1123/jtpe.28.1.90

Ovens, A., Smith, W., & Bowes, M. (2020). *MoveWell: Supporting children's learning and enjoyment of movement.* Sport New Zealand. Free download from https://penz.org.nz/movewell/

Patey, M., Yeonkyoung, J., Byoungwook A., Weon-Il, L., & Kyoung June, Y. (2023). Engaging in inclusive pedagogy: How elementary physical and health educators understand their roles. *International Journal of Inclusive Education*, 27(14), 1659–1678, https://doi.org/10.1080/13603116.2021.1916102

Roberts, J., & Bolstad, R. (2010). *Better than a professional? Students as co-contributors to educational design.* New Zealand Council for Educational Research. Retrieved from: https://ndhadeliver.natlib.govt.nz/delivery/DeliveryManagerServlet?dps_pid=IE25628004

Robinson, D.B., Borden, L.L. & Robinson, I.M. (2013). Charting a course for culturally responsive physical education. *Alberta Journal of Educational Research*, 58(4), 526–546. https://doi.org/10.11575/ajer.v58i4.55757

Timperley, H. (2022). Adaptive expertise and evaluative thinking in leadership and teaching. *Scan: The Journal for Educators*, 41(7), 21–24. https://search.informit.org/doi/10.3316/informit.797261906166518

Timperley, H., Kaser, L., & Halbert, J. (2014). *A framework for transforming learning in schools: Innovation and the spiral of inquiry: Seminar Series 234.* Centre for Strategic Education.

Valencia, R. R. (2010). *Dismantling contemporary deficit thinking: Educational thought and practice.* Routledge.

Wrench, A., & Garrett, R. (2021). Culturally responsive pedagogy in health and physical education. In J. Stirrup & O. Hooper (Eds.), *Critical pedagogies in physical education, physical activity and health* (pp.196–209). Routledge.

Young, S., & Sternod, B.M. (2011). Practicing culturally responsive pedagogy in Physical Education. *Journal of Modern Educational Review*, 1(1), 1–9. Retrieved from: https://ssrn.com/abstract=1963146

Suggestions of Additional Resources

- Bishop, R. (2019). *Teaching to the North-East: Relationship-based learning in practice*. NZCER Press.
- Baker, K., Scanlon, D., Tannehill, D., & Coulter, M. (2023). Teaching social justice through TPSR: where do I start? *Journal of Physical Education, Recreation & Dance, 94*(2), 11–18, https://doi.org/10.1080/07303084.2022.2146611
- Ovens, A., Smith, W., & Bowes, M. (2020). *MoveWell: Supporting children's learning and enjoyment of movement*. Sport New Zealand. Free download from https://penz.org.nz/movewell/
- Learning about meaningful Physical Education research project. https://meaningfulpe.wordpress.com/

Part III
The Structure of Social Pedagogy Programs as Physical Education Practice

6 Nurturing Activist Teachers in Physical Education Teacher Education

Carla Nascimento Luguetti and Mats Hordvik

Learning Objectives

At the end of this chapter, you will be able to:

- Describe the transformational journey teachers engage in becoming activist educators.
- Reflect upon Physical Education teacher education (PETE) practices to be used in nurturing activist educators.

VIGNETTE

When I started here [PETE programme], I thought that as a teacher we know everything. Learning an activist approach changed my life… I understood the importance of listening to the students… when I learned to really listen to them and understand their needs… what I changed is that I have a very strong connection with the kids and their parents. I changed as a teacher, and the way I'm going to teach from now on is the way I learned here (pre-service teacher's interview)

Introduction

Activist teachers are committed to social justice and attempt to promote deep changes in the *status quo* of Physical Education, sharing a commitment to equity, democracy, and social justice (Enright et al., 2018; Lynch & Ovens, 2022). They are simultaneously anti-capitalist (against class exploration), anti-imperialist (against colonisation), anti-patriarchal (against gender inequality), anti-racist (against White supremacy), anti-LGBTQI+ phobic and anti-ableism, and engage in a continuous process of transforming the status quo (Diniz-Pereira, 2013). The main intention of activist teachers is to construct a more just and humane society by critically analysing the conditions of oppression and collectively negotiating and/or changing the conditions together with students (Diniz-Pereira, 2013; Freire, 1987).

DOI: 10.4324/9781003411536-10

Working to change the status quo is a challenging endeavour, and researchers have, therefore, emphasised the importance of including social justice pedagogies in Physical Education teacher education (PETE) (Lynch et al., 2022; Ovens et al., 2018; Philpot, 2016; Walton-Fisette & Sutherland, 2018). In the last three decades, we have seen an increasing number of scholars arguing for social justice to be included in PETE. This body of research points to the potential of social justice pedagogies to enable teachers and students to take action for democracy and empowerment in PETE (Lynch et al., 2022). Pedagogies for social justice are committed to equity, democracy and have challenged and/or negotiated forms of discrimination in Physical Education (e.g., neoliberalism, sexism, racism and ableism) by interrogating and de-naturalising the conditions of oppression. There is a need for PETE programmes to incorporate social justice pedagogies better in order to nurture activist teachers in challenging the status quo in Physical Education (Lynch et al., 2022).

This chapter encourages reflection and discussion about PETE practices that nurture activist teachers. We begin by describing the main aspects of the learning journey of becoming an activist teacher: listening and trusting students, challenging stereotypes, and assumptions, and disrupting traditional power relations. Following this, we present five key practices to be considered in nurturing activist teachers in PETE: (i) *Acting against oppressive social injustices,* (ii) *Co-creating inclusive learning experiences,* (iii) *Encouraging reflection about positionality and privileges,* (iv) *Engaging in professional learning to continuously become activist teachers,* (v) *Modelling to be and become an activist teacher.* Figure 6.1 illustrates the connection between the main aspects of the learning journey and the five key practices in the continuous process of becoming an activist teacher. We argue that the suggested key practices (social justice pedagogies) have the potential to create spaces for nurturing activist teachers who can critically and continuously consider conditions of oppression and negotiate and/or change such conditions together with students.

While pre-service teachers (PSTs) and teacher educators are the key actors in traditional PETE, we believe PETE is a lifelong process that involves continuous professional learning for PSTs, in-service teachers and teacher educators. All teachers – that is, PSTs, in-service teachers, or teacher educators – are therefore encouraged to engage in a continuous process of becoming activist teachers, and the five practices can be used by all actors in different educational contexts (e.g., university-based PETE, continuous professional development for in-service teachers or teacher educators). Based on this view, in this chapter, we use the term 'teacher' to refer to both teacher educators, PSTs and in-service teachers, and specify if we find it needed to provide the reader with a clear sense of which context we refer to (e.g., schoolteacher and student, teacher educator and PST).

This chapter emphasises the transformative potential of pedagogy as a human-centred practice, particularly within the realm of social pedagogy. Grounded in the belief in the agency and freedom of all individuals, social

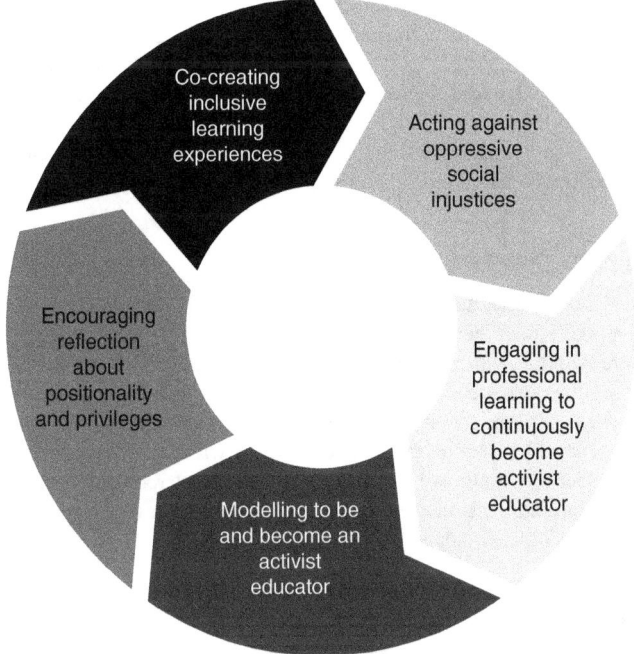

Figure 6.1 The key PETE practices in nurturing activist teachers in becoming an activist teacher.

pedagogy shifts its focus from those perceived as "in need" to individuals actively shaping and experiencing their lives. This perspective aligns with nurturing activist teachers in Physical Education who are committed to challenging the status quo and promoting social justice. The subsequent discussion outlines key practices essential for developing activist teachers, emphasising the importance of continuous professional learning for pre-service teachers, in-service teachers, and teacher educators. Further, it explores the potential contribution of critically informed understandings of social pedagogy in improving Physical Education praxis in a spirit of hope and human solidarity, aligning with the broader goal of nurturing activist teachers capable of challenging systemic inequalities.

The Transformative Journey of Becoming an Activist Teacher

As emphasised in the vignette, becoming an activist teacher requires an openness to transform ourselves in order to negotiate the challenges that arise in the process. We argue that this is a continuous process influenced by the conditions and relationships in the particular school and classroom. A teacher is not an activist teacher per se but needs to negotiate conditions in the classroom and their day-to-day practice. Teachers need to develop several skills and knowledge to become activist teachers. These include challenging stereotypes and assumptions about students, listening to and trusting students, and disrupting traditional power relationships in the classroom.

Challenging Stereotypes and Assumptions

To become activist teachers, teachers need to continuously engage in a personal struggle with their own stereotypes and assumptions about the people they are working with (McIntyre, 2003). For example, teachers working in socially vulnerable areas might believe that hard work and merit lead to success regardless of the social and cultural contexts (meritocracy). In that sense, students might be seen as the recipients of knowledge. To become activist teachers, teachers continually confront their personal stereotypes and assumptions of reinforcing the misconception that teachers are saviours and students are recipients of knowledge.

Listening and Trusting Students

Activist teachers need to listen to and talk with students to find a common language that facilitates dialogue. Listening to and trusting students is central to learning and becoming an activist teacher. This requires a special form of listening; one that not only requires open eyes and ears but also open hearts and minds (Delpit, 1988). For that, mutual respect and trust among teachers and students is essential. Mutual respect requires a learning community to be created in class (hooks, 1994) and can be developed over time in the context of relationships and/or relationship-building activities.

Disrupting Traditional Power Relations

To become activist teachers, teachers must work towards disrupting traditional power relationships in the classroom (Freire, 1987). Traditional power relationships reinforce the idea that teachers have the knowledge and should oversee all decisions; students in that sense are passive in receiving the information. Activist teachers need to learn how to break down power differentials so that students may experience the freedom to become critical thinkers and critical beings in the world (Freire, 2005). Such change is not always easy since it challenges conventional conceptions of students as subordinate to the teacher's expertise, and how they engage with what is taught and how.

Key PETE Practices in Nurturing Activist Teachers

In this section, we introduce some of the key practices or pedagogies PETE should consider in nurturing activist teachers.

Becoming Conscious about and Acting against Oppressive Social Injustices

Acting against oppressive social injustice resolves around the Freirean notions of consciousness and praxis (Freire, 1987). Consciousness focuses on developing an in-depth understanding the world allows for the perception and exposure of social and political flaws (Box 6.1). As Freire conceives it, consciousness involves individuals becoming critically aware of their own lived experiences, the social context in which they exist, and the systems of oppression that shape their reality.

Box 6.1 Becoming conscious about and acting against oppressive social injustices

Teacher educators could offer spaces where they together with PSTs so that they can recognize forms of oppression in their classrooms or 'the isms' such as healthism, fatism, ableism and elitism, genderism and sexism, heterosexism, racism, classism, linguicism, and colonialism (for more information see Lynch et al., 2022). Here are some ways to implement this in PETE programmes:

> Incorporate sessions dedicated to examining various forms of oppression and 'isms' within the PETE curriculum.
> Encourage dialogue that allows teacher educators and PSTs to share their experiences, questions, and concerns about these 'isms.'
> Use real-life case studies and scenarios to illustrate how these forms of oppression can manifest in Physical Education settings.

It is a prerequisite for engaging in praxis because individuals must first understand the issues and inequities they wish to address before taking action (Freire, 1987). Praxis refers to taking informed and reflective action to change oppressive systems and social conditions. It involves the dynamic interplay between action and reflection (Box 6.1). Praxis is guided by critical consciousness; individuals critically reflect on their experiences and the social context to inform their actions and engage in meaningful, transformative change (Freire, 1987).

Co-creating Inclusive Learning Experiences

The second key practice is related to involving students as co-contributors in the classroom (Box 6.2). Activist teachers invite students to co-create a curriculum that is inclusive and meaningful for all. Understanding teaching and learning as a collaborative process and students as knowledgeable partners creates a space where students feel empowered and motivated to participate in their own learning experience (Cook-Sather, 2002). It is important to highlight that although students might participate in different forms, their participation cannot be tokenistic in the classroom (Bovill et al., 2011; Cook-Sather et al., 2014). There is a need to reposition the learner as a subject of pedagogy so that learners are involved in the educational process of producing a course that is meaningful, inclusive, and relevant to their lives (Lynch & Ovens, 2021).

Box 6.2 Co-creating inclusive learning experiences

There are diverse forms in which PSTs might participate as co-contributors in the classroom. For example, PSTs' participation can take forms such as (a) 'PSTs as Co-creators of Teaching Approaches' where teachers educators and PSTs engage in reflective dialogue about what is happening and what could be happening in classrooms; (b) 'PSTs as Co-creators of Course Design' where teacher educators and PSTs experiment a variety of approaches to partnering in 'course design teams' that co-create or re-create, a course; and (c) 'PSTs as Co-creators of Curricula' where teacher educators and PSTs co-create the entire curricula. Here are some ways to implement this in PETE programmes:

> Organise regular reflective dialogue sessions between teacher educators and PSTs to discuss classroom experiences by encouraging PSTs to share their observations, questions, and ideas about teaching and learning.
>
> Collaboratively plan lessons with PSTs, allowing them to contribute their insights and suggestions for teaching strategies, materials, and assessments.
>
> Course design teams comprising teacher educators and PSTs can co-create or re-create course content, assignments, and assessments together.
>
> Create advisory curriculum committees that include PSTs as active members. Allow them to contribute to decisions about course offerings, program structure, and educational goals.

Encouraging Reflection about Positionality and Privileges

The third key practice is encouraging reflection about positionality and privileges. Teachers may have power and privilege from their class, education, racial/ethnic backgrounds, gender, sexuality, or other identity positions, and continuous reflection about their power and privilege functions as a prerequisite to becoming an activist teacher. Reflection becomes key in transforming some of the power relations in classrooms and requires consideration of questions related to who, what and how of teaching and learning.

This encourages teachers to reflect upon the uniqueness of each classroom and student and acknowledge that there is no one way of being an activist teacher or that certain socially just pedagogies are appropriate with all students/classes, but that they instead need to adapt to the particular context – that is, the social conditions, the curriculum, the classroom, the students on a day-to-day basis (Box 6.3). As emphasised in the opening vignette, when teachers start to listen to their students and understand their needs, they also develop a solid connection with them and their families.

Box 6.3 Encouraging reflection about positionality and privilege

Teachers need to be self-reflexive about their positionality and privileges, and continuously ask: *Who am I? Who are the students? What are some of my privileges? How does my positionality influence my teaching? What are the assumptions I have about the students I am working with?* Here are some ways to implement this in PETE programmes:

Require PSTs to keep reflective journals that document their thoughts, reactions, and personal experiences related to their positionality and privileges.

Assign collaborative projects that require PSTs to work together to examine their own beliefs, biases, and values. These projects can include curriculum development or community engagement initiatives.

Engaging in Professional Learning to Continuously Become Activist Teachers

Professional learning is the fourth key practice in nurturing activist teachers (Box 6.4). Teachers who engage in practices of professional learning acknowledge that being an activist teacher is not something you are but something you continuously are becoming about others. Professional learning can involve collaborative practices (learning communities, collective pedagogical projects, group practice) and take forms of practitioner enquiry (e.g., self-study, action research, lesson study) (Gonçalves et al., 2022). Such practices can encourage teachers to reflect on their individual pedagogical practices and underlying beliefs and assumptions about teaching and learning and develop reflexivity and challenging taken-for-granted practices.

Box 6.4 Engaging in professional learning to continuously become activist teachers

Teachers can be encouraged to participate in professional learning that involves collaborative practices and practitioner enquiry to becoming activist teachers. PSTs form learning communities where they collaborate with peers to explore and discuss issues related to Physical Education. Collaborative practices and practitioner enquiry could also be extended to teacher educators and schoolteachers in school-university partnerships. Here are some ways to implement this in PETE programmes:

PSTs engage in co-teaching experiences, working in pairs or small groups to plan and implement lessons. This collaborative practice allows for shared responsibilities and mutual support.

PSTs conduct action research projects to investigate specific teaching and learning challenges in Physical Education. They collect data, analyse results, and make informed changes to their instructional practices based on their findings.

PSTs, teacher educators and schoolteachers participate in collaborative meetings to investigate challenges they face during school placement.

Modelling to Be and Become an Activist Teacher

Modelling is the final key practice in nurturing activist teachers. It encourages teachers to engage in the journey and practice actively and consistently as they advocate for others. In essence, teachers must recognise that 'how they teach' (Russel, 1997) and 'who they are in how they teach' (Keltchermans, 2009) is the message they send to students. Therefore, we argue that modelling encompasses the journey of becoming an activist teacher and the other key practices for nurturing activist teachers, fostering an ongoing commitment to embody the practices of always becoming activist teachers.

Box 6.5 Modelling to be and become an activist teacher

PETE programmes can model social justice practices by creating a programme that not only teaches about social justice but also embodies these principles throughout its structure and processes. This 'practice what you preach' approach not only prepares future Physical Education teachers to promote social justice but also reinforces the importance of these principles in education. Here are some ways to implement this in PETE programmes:

> Encourage teacher educators to engage in ongoing self-reflection about their own teaching practices and biases and share some of these reflections with PSTs. This modelling of self-awareness sets an example for PSTs and facilitates future reflection and discussion.
>
> As a teacher educator, model inclusive language and respectful communication in all interactions with PSTs. Use gender-inclusive pronouns and language that acknowledges diverse identities.
>
> During practicum, model inclusive and culturally responsive teaching practices by emphasising strategies that meet the needs of all students, regardless of their abilities or backgrounds.

Advice from the Field

How would you describe the concept of an "activist teacher" in Physical Education, and what role do you think activist teachers can play in promoting social justice and equity within the classroom?

Martine Simonsen (Norway, schoolteacher): An activist teacher in Physical Education is a teacher who cares about students and aims to create justice and equity for all students. I believe it's essential to be a teacher who reflects on and acts in accordance with social justice to contribute to this for students. In addition, I think it's important to take specific actions in the classroom to promote social justice and equity. For example, it could be addressing students' individual needs, discussing and reflecting with students on social justice, and continually working to build meaningful relationships with students.

As a schoolteacher overseeing PSTs, how do you think their placements can contribute to their journey in becoming activist educators? Are there specific experiences or practices you encourage during these placements?

Martine Simonsen (Norway, schoolteacher): I think the placement period can contribute to making PSTs more aware of what it means to become activist teachers, but this requires that the placement teachers focus on and discuss the topic with PSTs. It is important that students learn how to promote equity in specific situations during their placement experience. With the right guidance, PSTs can gain knowledge that they will carry forward into their future careers. During the placement periods, I focus on having a good dialogue with students about how they can become activist teachers. I encourage them to try to build relationships with students and accept differences among students. Another important practice I engage in is discussing specific situations with PSTs that either positively or negatively affected students' experiences of equity and social justice. This helps PSTs become more aware of and encourage reflection on how such situations could be addressed in the best interest of the students.

In your experience, how can PSTs effectively confront their own stereotypes and assumptions about students while on placement, and what support can schoolteachers provide in this regard?

Martine Simonsen (Norway, schoolteacher): All PSTs will have some assumptions about the students they are going to meet during their placements. All students are different, and it is important for PSTs to encounter a diversity of students. By actively trying to get to know and understand different students, I believe PSTs are confronted with their own stereotypes. School teachers can be clear that all students have different backgrounds and needs, provide concrete examples, and encourage PSTs to reflect on their assumptions. For example, how to include students from minority backgrounds or with disabilities in their teaching.

What strategies have you found effective in co-creating inclusive learning experiences with PSTs, and how does this align with the goal of nurturing activist educators?

Martine Simonsen (Norway, schoolteacher): I have found that the most effective ways to create inclusive learning experiences in collaboration with PSTs are to make them aware of the importance of social justice in teaching, discuss the topic and specific situations with PSTs, and provide them with enough knowledge and tools to promote social justice. One challenge I have experienced in Norway is that the placement period is rather short (2-6 weeks), so it can be difficult for PSTs to actually build good relationships with students. However, with the right focus on promoting equality and social justice, as well as discussing important situations related to this in practice, I believe placement teachers lay a good foundation for PSTs to develop as activist educators.

Key Points

This chapter discusses the concept of nurturing activist teachers in PETE. Activist teachers are committed to social justice and aim to challenge the status quo in Physical Education. The chapter outlines the main aspects of the journey towards becoming an activist teacher and suggests five key practices for nurturing activist teachers in PETE:

- *Acting against Oppressive Social Injustices*: Teachers need to develop a deep understanding of social and political flaws and engage in informed and reflective action to address oppressive systems.
- *Co-Creating Inclusive Learning Experiences*: Involving students as co-contributors in the classroom and recognising them as knowledgeable partners empowers students to participate actively in their own learning.
- *Encouraging Reflection about Positionality and Privileges*: Reflection is crucial for teachers to understand their own power and privilege and to transform power dynamics in the classroom.
- *Engaging in Professional Learning*: Continuous professional learning is essential for teachers to develop reflexivity and challenge ingrained practices.
- *Modelling to Be and Become an Activist Teacher*: Teacher educators need to model social justice principles and practices in their own programmes to reinforce the importance of these principles.

This chapter underscores the lifelong nature of becoming an activist teacher and encourages all teachers, including PSTs, in-service teachers, and teacher educators, to engage in this continuous process. It concludes by highlighting the importance of PETE programmes committing to equity, democracy, and social justice in nurturing activist educators.

Reflection Questions and Activities

1 Can you share any personal experiences or insights about how confronting your own stereotypes and assumptions about students can be a challenging yet crucial aspect of becoming an activist teacher?
2 Why is active listening and building trust with students considered central to the journey of becoming an activist teacher, and how do these practices contribute to more inclusive and equitable learning environments?
3 In what ways can disrupting traditional power relations in the classroom empower students and contribute to their critical thinking and engagement in the learning process?
4 How can teacher effectively model social justice principles in PETE programmes, and why is the idea of 'practicing what you preach' important in nurturing activist teachers?

References

Bovill, C., Cook-Sather, A., & Felten, P. (2011). Students as co-creators of teaching approaches, course design and curricula: Implications for academic developers. *International Journal for Academic Development, 16*(2), 133–145. https://doi.org/10.1080/1360144X.2011.568690

Cook-Sather, A. (2002). Authorizing students' perspectives: toward trust, dialogue, and change in education. *Educational Researcher, 31*(4), 3–14. https://doi.org/10.3102/0013189X031004003

Cook-Sather, A., Bovill, C., & Felten, P. (2014). *Engaging students as partners in learning and teaching: A guide for faculty*. John Wiley & Sons Inc.

Delpit, L.D. (1988). The silenced dialogue: Power and pedagogy in educating other people's children. *Harvard Educational Review, 58*(3), 19. http://lmcreadinglist.pbworks.com/f/Delpit+(1988).pdf

Diniz-Pereira, J. (2013). *How the dreamers are born: Struggles for social justice and the identity construction of activist educators in Brazil*. Peter Lang Publishing.

Enright, E., Williams, B., Sperka, L., & Peucker, K. (2018). Pedagogic rights and the acoustics of health and physical education teacher education: Whose voices are heard? *Physical Education and Sport Pedagogy, 23*(5), 524–535. https://doi.org/10.1080/17408989.2018.1470616

Freire, P. (1987). *Pedagogia do oprimido [Pedagogy of the oppressed]* (17th ed.). Paz e Terra.

Freire, P. (2005). *Teachers as cultural workers: Letters to those who dare teach*. Westview Press.

Gonçalves, L.L., Luguetti, C., & Borges, C. (2022). Collaborative continuing professional development in physical education: an introduction. *Movimento, 28*(e28063), 1–11. https://doi.org/10.22456/1982-8918.127919

Hooks, b. (1994). *Teaching to transgress: Education as the practice of freedom*. Routledge.

Kelchtermans, G. (2009). Who I am in how I teach is the message: self-understanding, vulnerability and reflection. *Teachers and Teaching*, 15(2), 257–272. https://doi.org/10.1080/13540600902875332

Lynch, S., Ovens, A. (2021). Critical Pedagogy in Physical Education. In: Peters, M.A. (eds) Encyclopedia of Teacher Education. Springer, *Singapore*. https://doi.org/10.1007/978-981-13-1179-6_417-1

Lynch, S., Walton-Fisette, J.L., & Luguetti, C. (2022). *Pedagogies of social justice in physical education and youth sport*. Routledge.

McIntyre, A. (2003). Participatory action research and urban education: Reshaping the teacher preparation process. *Equity & Excellence in Education, 36*(1), 28–39. https://doi.org/10.1080/10665680303497

Ovens, A., Flory, S.B., Sutherland, S., Philpot, R., Walton-Fisette, J.L., Hill, J., Phillips, S., & Flemons, M. (2018). How PETE comes to matter in the performance of social justice education. *Physical Education and Sport Pedagogy, 23*(5), 484–496. https://doi.org/10.1080/17408989.2018.1470614

Philpot, R. (2016). Physical education initial teacher educators' expressions of critical pedagogy(ies). *European Physical Education Review, 22*(2), 260–275. https://doi.org/10.1177/1356336x15603382

Russell T. (1997). Teaching teachers: How I teach IS the message. In: J. Loughran & T. Russell (Eds.) Teaching about teaching: Purpose, *passion and pedagogy in teacher education*, pp. 32–47. London: Falmer Press.

Walton-Fisette, J.L., & Sutherland, S. (2018). Moving forward with social justice education in physical education teacher education. *Physical Education and Sport Pedagogy, 23*(5), 461–468. https://doi.org/10.1080/17408989.2018.1476476

7 Social Pedagogy and Model-Based Approaches in Physical Education

Kanae Haneishi, Tse Sheng Teng, Bruce Nkala, Korey Boyd, Linda Griffin and Mauro Andre

Learning Objectives

At the end of this chapter, you will be able to:

- Explain key components when developing Physical Education lesson plans using Game-Based Approaches (GBA) as an example of Model-Based Approaches (MBA) to implement social pedagogy concepts.
- Effectively modify games to address Justice, Equity Diversity, and Inclusion (JEDI) during daily Physical Education lessons.
- Ask intentional questions to guide students to think critically and engage in critical dialogue during a GBA lesson.

VIGNETTE

Julia is in the middle of a 2v2 soccer game in her Physical Education class. She is a very active ten-year-old. Physical Education is the highlight of her week as she gets to play with her friends. Julia is very proficient in soccer, but her group stopped the game as they noticed that Johnny could not keep up with the group. After a brief discussion with and support from, their teacher, they agreed that the opposing team could not steal the ball from Johnny (block his shots and passes) and that Julia (the most skilled player) could only have five touches on the ball. The game resumed, and the new rules improved their overall experience. Julia felt more challenged, and Johnny felt more included and engaged.

Within the same class, Cody has a solid repertoire of fundamental motor skills but has strong ideals of gendered movement expressions. This leads him to view game modifications as not being masculine or something designated for low-skilled students. After a brief discussion with the class, the teacher directs students to rotate to the nearby group. Julia and Johnny now find themselves in a group with Cody, a skilled student who struggles to value and appreciate modified or small-sided games. Cody often refers to them as "not real games" or "gym games". Students agree that the opposing team could not steal the ball from Johnny because he is the least skilled student in this new group and that Cody and Julia (the most skilled players) could only have three touches on the ball per possession. The game resumed, and the rules increased the overall complexity of the task. As before, Julia felt challenged; however, Cody's attitude worsened during this task.

Introduction

Model-based approaches (MBA) have provided teachers with clear frameworks and an explicit way to plan instruction for the past 30 years in Physical Education. MBA intentionally focus on transforming instruction into pedagogy through purposeful accommodation of learner's needs across all three domains (i.e., cognitive, psychomotor, and affective) (Casey & Kirk, 2020; Ennis, 2015; Metzler & Colquitt, 2021). MBA also help to address the range of students' ability (Metzler & Colquitt, 2021) and make learning environments more diverse and inclusive. An effective curriculum model has

> a comprehensive and coherent plan for teaching that includes a theoretical foundation, clearly stated learning outcomes, teachers' needed content knowledge expertise, developmentally appropriate and sequenced learning activities, expectations for teacher and students' behaviours, unique task structures, measures of learning outcomes, and mechanism for verifying the faithful implementation of the model itself.
>
> (Metzler & Colquitt, 2021, p. 9)

Various MBA in Physical Education have been introduced to provide a focused and theme-based framework about how Physical Education teachers design and deliver specific units. Indicative examples are Teaching Games for Understanding (as a model proposed for teaching games) (Bunker & Thorpe, 1982), Sport Education (Siedentop et al., 2020), Teaching Personal and Social Responsibility (TPSR) (Hellison, 2011), Skill theme approach (Holt/Hale, 2015), Adventure Education (Dyson & Sutherland, 2015), and Cultural Studies (O'Sullivan et al., 2015).

Game Based Approaches (GBA) to Physical Education teaching and sports coaching have attracted significant attention both from theoretical and pedagogical perspectives over the years of their implementation. GBA are a form of 'learner-centred teaching and coaching practice in which the modified small-sided games set the base and framework for developing thoughtful, creative, intelligent, and skilful players' (AIESEP TGfU Special Interest Group, 2023). These modified games are situated as learning opportunities followed by discussions to enhance critical thinking. As suggested in the opening vignette, critical thinking is rather important since some students may hold gendered movement expressions, which leads them to treat low-skilled students as inferior to them during their participation in games and game activities. GBA utilise constructivism as a theoretical underpinning educational philosophy within games teaching and learning. Constructivism promotes 'comprehension and meaning be built gradually using experiences and contexts that help students become willing and able to learn' (Butler & McCahan, 2005, p. 35). As such, within GBA, students become problem-solvers and critical thinkers, while teachers play the role of facilitator. GBA involve a process of self-discovering, identifying what we do not know and applying what we know, setting its focus on decision-making rather than solely focusing on performance (Butler & McCahan, 2005). Due to their unique characteristics of game modification and questioning, this chapter uses GBA as a form of model-based practice to apply the concept of social pedagogy. We believe that GBA have the potential for creating socially oriented Physical Education lessons and establishing the relationship between motivating content (games), specifically modified game rules (situated learning) and constructivist-oriented discussions (students as critical thinkers). This chapter addresses how to deliver socially oriented Physical Education lessons using GBA.

Social Pedagogy and Game-Based Approaches

As you recall from Chapter 2, the authors outline three basic principles that guide social pedagogy: (1) students are the centre of teachers' work, with teachers working with students through co-constructed activities, (2) interpersonal relationships are mediators of teaching and learning, and (3) and students are encouraged to embrace their own learning journey. GBA align meaningfully to social pedagogy since game situations combine these three principles. Since games are social, public, and dynamic, there are many teaching moments and learning experiences for Physical Education teachers to address important social and life skills during game teaching (e.g., communication skills, leadership skills, conflict resolution skills, and civic engagement). Using games and game forms is essential to GBA in Physical Education. Students are at the centre of GBA lessons and are the agents of deliberative and democratic living (Hämäläinen, 2012), who can transfer what they learned in Physical Education into the community and society. Therefore, GBA provide an educational venue for Physical Education teachers to address social issues and promote various educational aims of social pedagogy, such as democracy, social inclusion, participation, social development, social skills, communicative culture, active citizenship, and citizen morals (Hämäläinen, 2012).

We are currently living in a society where we have frequently witnessed numerous incidents related to inequity and discrimination as well as racial and social injustices. In school settings, students of this generation face a wide variety of challenges, such as cyberbullying, school shootings, mental health, and an increase in suicide attempts/deaths (Mitchell & Walton-Fisette, 2022). Physical Education professionals have addressed the importance of promoting equity, diversity, and inclusion and have called for meaningful changes for social justice in Physical Education (Block et al., 2021; Culp, 2021; Haneishi et al., 2023a, 2023b; Lynch et al., 2021).

Historically, GBA promote humanistic values in game teaching and learning. Butler (2016, p. 55) states that the GBA curriculum "values the ability to work cooperatively and make smart, democratic decisions as much as it does the performance of physical skills". In GBA teaching methodologies, the teacher facilitates interactions in a naturalistic setting and unpacks the social dynamics and complexities that games offer and have the potential to increase students' emotional, cognitive, and social awareness, and engagement as they discuss, and problem-solve within the playing of the game (Mitchell et al., 2021). Using pedagogical principles, such as modifying and adapting games and teachers facilitating critical dialogue and problem-solving as co-constructed activities (e.g., team discussions), GBA offer a space for Physical Education teachers and students to reflect on important social issues in small group activities. Students who are taught using GBA are given opportunities to create a space where they discuss, problem solve (i.e., adjusting rules for inclusion and equity), and collaborate with each other. We have all witnessed incidents, like the one described in the opening vignette, when students misbehave or have problems in working together due to inappropriately selected game rules and constraints. Alternatively, in cases when Physical Education teachers plan and deliver lessons that are carefully and intentionally designed to infuse Justice, Equity, Diversity, and Inclusion (JEDI) concepts, the GBA classroom context can promote learning experiences where differences such as race, age, gender, (dis)ability, and ethnicity are addressed. The game learning space becomes inclusive, equitable, and justice for all students. In this case, the Physical Education learning environment may promote critical life skills important for the upbringing of students as global and community citizens (i.e., social skills, active citizenship and citizen morals, social inclusion, and social development).

Therefore, this chapter focuses on promoting Justice, Equity, Diversity, and Inclusion (JEDI) using GBA as a social pedagogical framework in Physical Education. While using GBA, Physical Education teachers may create a learning environment that "places importance on work with the whole child, broad developmental goals, interactivity with peers and educators and quality of life" (Moss, 2007, p. 18) and supports "the child's meaning-making acquired through relationships and experience of the world" (Moss, 2007,

p. 18). The chapter provides practical examples of how Physical Education teachers can deliver GBA as an inclusive and socially oriented pedagogy that aims "for greater/more meaningful participation in society by helping children develop confidence and/or other emotional, practical and social skills" (Rothuizen & Harbo, 2017).

Soccer Lesson Flow to Address JEDI Using a Social Pedagogy Framework

In the proceeding section, we will illustrate how to implement a social pedagogy framework and address JEDI in game teaching and learning. To apply social pedagogy concepts during a GBA lesson with a JEDI perspective, Physical Education teachers need to intentionally modify (i.e., exaggeration and representation) games and define a line of questioning purposefully designed with these intentions (Bunker & Thorpe, 1982). Table 7.1 shows the basic GBA lesson structure and highlights the alignment of discrete lesson parameters with social pedagogy principles.

As shown in Figure 7.1, within GBA the lesson is an ongoing teaching cycle that enables the teacher and students to engage in co-constructed activities through the social nature of games. Each game or game form sets up a problem-solving activity in which students work through solutions that can cut across any learning domains (i.e., psychomotor, cognitive, or affective). These solutions rely on the teacher and students' interpersonal relationships as an essential part of the learning process. The goal is to improve gameplay and develop students to become more informed and competent game players while developing problem-solving skills and the ability to think critically. Each process of problem, solution and learning in games teaching may encompass an array of social pedagogy principles when the teacher decides to infuse JEDI issues within the lesson.

Table 7.2 is an example of a soccer lesson flow designed with GBA pedagogical principles to teach the tactical and technical components of the game while reinforcing a JEDI social perspective. The lesson targeted grades 9–12 (age 14–17); however, Physical Education teachers can use this same example and modify it based on their students' physical, cognitive, and psychosocial development. The lesson focus is "promoting JEDI whilst teaching about maintaining possession of the ball in soccer". The lesson objectives are:

Psychomotor: Students can make an accurate pass to a teammate to maintain possession of the ball for 70% of the playing time.
Cognitive: Students will be able to list three important strategies to establish as a team to maintain the possession of the ball.
Affective: Students can include all teammates and respect diversity and equity through just discussions.

Table 7.1 Alignment to address JEDI issues by using a social pedagogy framework

Lesson structure of GBA	Social pedagogy principles
Students engaged in modified games begin each lesson.	Students are the centre of a teacher's work (i.e., social learning view). Teachers work with students through co-constructed activities.
Students discuss the games played to help gain an understanding of ways to improve the game – in-game knowledge, and about game knowledge.	Teachers facilitate and students are encouraged to embrace their own learning.
Students practise skills and movements – situational practice.	Interpersonal relationships are mediators of teaching and learning.
Students return to a modified game thus reaching full circle (i.e., play & discussions, practice and play).	Interpersonal relationships are mediators of teaching and learning. Teachers facilitate and students are encouraged to embrace their own learning.

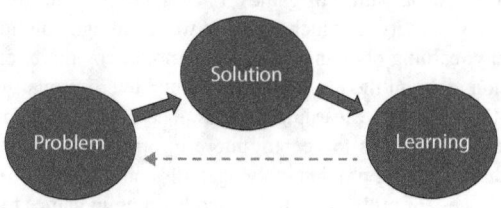

Figure 7.1 Simplified flow of games based approaches.

Conclusion

This chapter provides a practical example of how GBA – as a form of model-based practice (MBA) – can be used to deliver a Physical Education lesson from a social pedagogy perspective. Games are social, have structure, and rely on relationships to work (i.e., teammates, opponents, officials). These three social pedagogy principles can foster dialogue and understanding of justice, equity, diversity, and inclusion from a socio-cultural perspective. That was why among various MBA, we particularly focused on GBA and attempted to highlight how this approach can help promote some of the critical social and life skills in daily Physical Education lessons.

Social Pedagogy and Model-Based Approaches 95

Table 7.2 Indicative example of lesson flow

Anticipated progression of tasks	How task will be communicated & instructional cues	Organisational arrangements – Instructional strategy and social pedagogical principles
Game 1: 4 v 4 Keep Away Games	Teacher Explanation	The focus on creating opportunities to learn together as a team is an intentional design in GBA.
Two teams (4 v 4)	Task Presentation	This is aligned to social pedagogy's intent to create a strong sense of community.
• The goal is to try to keep the ball away from the other team as long as possible by passing the ball among teammates.	Demonstration	
• 5 passes = 1 point		
• Max of 3 touches (to emphasise "passing")		
• Cold/warm/hot defences		
• Possession change:		
1 intercept and		
2 ball out of the bounce		
• The purpose of the game is to make a good decision and make accurate passes to possess the ball as a team		
Question & Discussion 1		
Topic: **Three main points of possessing the ball as a team.**		
1 moving to open space		Group-oriented work is an important strategy for social pedagogic interventions
2 improving communication		
3 making accurate passes		
Question (Q):	Teacher Initiated Discussion	Critical Thinking
"What do we need to do in order to maintain the possession of the ball as a team?"		Listening to others' ideas
Expected Answer (EA):		
"moving to open space"		
"Talking to each other (i.e., communication)"		
"Controlling the ball and passing the ball with accuracy"		

(Continued)

Table 7.2 (Continued)

Anticipated progression of tasks	How task will be communicated & instructional cues	Organisational arrangements – Instructional strategy and social pedagogical principles
Correct Answers (the answers that teachers aim to guide the students to) *Maintaining Possession* 1 moving to open space 2 improving communication 3 making accurate passes **Question & Discussion 2** Topic: **Inclusion and Diversity** (from JEDI concept) "In order to be successful as a team it is important to include everyone on the team". Q: *"Is the game inclusive? What makes you say that?" "Why is it important to include everyone?"* *"What are additional rules that we should add while still focusing on maintaining possession?"* EA: *"Everyone needs to touch the ball before getting a point"* EA: *"You cannot pass back to the same teammate"* EA: *"Making the grid bigger"* *"Let's decide to add one of the suggested rules"*	Make observations not judgements in your dialogue with students. (Critical discussion) Emphasising on the importance of inclusion as well as diverse ideas/abilities (e.g., everyone can contribute to the team)	• Communication skills (i.e., listening skill, recognising diverse ideas and accepting ideas that are different from yours) • The intentional design to integrate the body, mind, emotions, and spirit through games and critical conversation. • Provide care, assistance, empowerment, and supervision to mobilise children and youth to adopt a certain way of thinking or acting. • Use relational approaches that promote independence and interdependence. • Facilitate learners to develop empathetic understandings as they develop construct or (re) orient ways of being and living with others.
Game 2: A keep away game (4 v 4) with one additional rule from students. The same game as Game 2 with adding "You cannot pass back to the same teammate".	Continue emphasising on three key points for maintaining possession.	The teacher intentionally chooses one idea from students and has students play under the *same* rule, and then the game leads to the next step of teaching equality vs. equity.

Social Pedagogy and Model-Based Approaches 97

Anticipated progression of tasks	How task will be communicated & instructional cues	Organisational arrangements – Instructional strategy and social pedagogical principles
Question & Group discussion 3 Topic: **Equity and Diversity** (from a JEDI perspective) Q: *"How was the experience? Was the game more inclusive after the change in rule?"* EA: *"Not quite. The game kept breaking down with the added rule. Our friends are still not getting the ball"*. Q: *"How can we have additional rules to provide individual support they need so ALL players can play this game more effectively; without causing the game to break down?"* *"Discuss as a group (if the number is small) or as a team (if the number is large)"*. EA: *"Lower skilled players can take more than 3 touches"*. *(Each team can decide 1-2 players who can touch unlimited touches.)"* EA: *"Creating a safe space where players can enter and have unlimited touches with no defender entering"*.	Explain the difference between "equality and equity" Emphasis on the importance of diverse ideas Goal: To value diverse ideas and promote equity, each team is allowed to decide one additional rule that they are applying to make the game more equitable.	• Use a values-led approach to supporting the development of children and young people, through relationship-centred practices. • Apply relational strategies that strive towards the understanding of other people. • Practitioners and individuals come together to negotiate decisions and roles.
Game 3: A keep away game (4 v 4) with another additional rule decided by each team. Topic: Equity	Playing the same rule while adding a new rule decided by each group. **Goal:** Continue emphasising on three key points for maintaining possession	• Explain the difference between "equality and equity" • Emphasis on the importance of diverse ideas • Each group discusses and decides the additional rule that is unique to the team based on individuals on the team.

(Continued)

Table 7.2 (Continued)

Anticipated progression of tasks	How task will be communicated & instructional cues	Organisational arrangements – Instructional strategy and social pedagogical principles
Practice Task Modification ideas: • If it is hard, make the distance shorter, use a smaller gate, or perform partner passing without a gate. • If it is easy, add progression. For example, place random gates around the space, and have students pass to a moving partner while moving.	Teaching some movement cues to make an accurate pass with inside of the foot (inside kick): • point planter foot to the target • lock your ankle of the kicking foot • degree contact with the ball • follow through to the target	To make this section more fun and challenging, students pass through a gate. The size of the gate can be decided by the students. □..⚽...pass......□ ▲ ▲ Students pair up and practise passing skills and trapping skills.
Game 4: Play the same game as Game 4 *This game can be similar to more an actual soccer game, such as adding goals Goal: Continue emphasising three key points for maintaining possession	Students go back to the keep away game focusing on all aspects (three key points of maintaining possession as well as passing skills).	Explaining the difference between "equality and equity" Emphasising on the importance of diverse ideas

Social Pedagogy and Model-Based Approaches 99

Anticipated progression of tasks	How task will be communicated & instructional cues	Organisational arrangements – Instructional strategy and social pedagogical principles
		Seek to guide and help people to shape or change their mentalities so as to act in a respectful, equitable and satisfactory level, when it comes to real life problems
Final Critical Reflection JEDI Questions (indicative): Q: "What are three key points of maintaining possession as a team?" • Did you include all teammates in the discussion? • Did you listen to everyone's idea? • How did your group choose the process of making decisions? • What is consensus building? • Who took the most power in making these decisions? • Who benefited? Who did not? • How does this help people of different abilities play together? • How does this help us to engage with our opponent? • Can someone explain what the team did? Where did the idea come from? • Did everyone agree on this? How did your group make decisions? • Can you think of an incident at home (or your community) when you were not included? How did you feel? • Do you think it is important for us to always try to include everyone/ listen to different perspectives? What makes you say that? • What is one thing you commit to do by next week to be more inclusive/ be a better listener? For example…	Inclusion Leadership skills	

......
**These are possible questions that the PE teacher can ask. The teacher needs to choose a few questions from here, not all. Some questions can be done in journal writings.

Advice from the Field

We have spent time thinking through how to integrate Justice, Equity, Diversity and Inclusion (JEDI) into a games-based model. We have approached our journey through a praxis lens to help us explore what works, what does not and why. As you begin your journey, we offer two pieces of advice to make this work:

1 Remain curious, be open and intentional.
2 Continue to learn, explore, and grow.

Remain Curious, Open and Intentional

As Physical Education teachers, we are creative individuals with an art to adapt lessons to enhance students' experience and learning across the multidimensionality and complexity of our classrooms (i.e., gymnasiums, outdoor fields, and pitches). As teachers, we talk about the teachable moments which offer a scenario in that moment (i.e., not planned) when you see something and facilitate a discussion at that moment. These moments provide us with the opportunity to address social issues and relationships as they arise (e.g., like addressing inclusion when students are excluding others during a game). As you explore these moments over time, these types of teachable moments help build your knowledge and skills and guide your students' understanding of JEDI concepts.

Start Simple, Learn, and Grow

Through our own praxis journey, we established a mindset of start simple, learn, and grow. Integrating JEDI concepts will be challenging. Therefore, we strongly urge you:

- Start simple with one concept (e.g., equity). We advocate that you choose a concept you can embrace and/or one in which you have observed unjust practices over and over.
- Learn and grow. JEDI work does not come without learning and with learning comes growing pains. Teachers need to be mindful with respect to their learning and growth related to JEDI concepts. When teachers are mindful, they can focus on developing their own awareness. By doing so, they will be able to calmly acknowledge thoughts and feelings in a thoughtful way and be able to embrace

> the discomfort and be patient with their students. As you learn and grow as a teacher, so do your students.
>
> We encourage you to explore the JEDI concepts through models-based instruction such as a game-based approach (e.g., tactical games model). Each instructional model provides a clear and intentional path for a teacher to begin taking the risks as you integrate JEDI concepts into your curriculum. As we know as teachers, we teach for the "long game" and "long game" here is a more open and patient society.

Key Points

Game-Based Approaches, one of the Model-Based Approaches, provide practical tools for Physical Education teachers to implement social pedagogy and address social issues around justice, equity, diversity, and inclusion in today's world.

Proper game-modifications and effective questioning are some of the key teaching techniques when teacher intends to address social issues and teach social skills during game teaching.

Reflection Questions and Activities

1 How can Game-Based Approaches (GBA) be used effectively to develop students' social skills that are critical as a member of a community?
2 What are some examples of game modifications when addressing diversity and inclusion in the society during a basketball game teaching?
3 List five example questions that can be used in your own teaching setting when addressing justice, equity, diversity, and inclusion in Physical Education.

References

AIESEP TGfU Special Interest Group. (2023, May 9). *Game-based consensus statement.* Teaching Games for Understanding. Retrieved from: http://www.tgfu.info/

Block, B.A., Haneishi, K., Zarco, E., & Megías, E.P. (2021). Thirdspace movement concepts in Physical Education Teacher Education. *Quest, 73*(4), 323–341. https://doi.org/10.1080/00336297.2021.1957691

Bunker, D., & Thorpe, R. (1982). A model for the teaching of games in the secondary school. *Bulletin of Physical Education, 10,* 9–16.

Butler, J. (2016). *Playing fair: Using student-invented games to prevent bullying, teach democracy, and promote social justice.* Human Kinetics.

Butler, J., & McCahan, B.J. (2005). Teaching games for understanding as a curriculum model. In L. Griffin & J. Butler (Eds.), *Teaching games for understanding: Theory, research and practice* (pp. 33–54). Human Kinetics.
Casey, A., & Kirk, D. (2020). *Models-based practice in physical education*. Routledge.
Culp, B. (2021). Everyone matters: eliminating dehumanizing practices in Physical Education. *JOPERD: The Journal of Physical Education, Recreation & Dance, 92*(1), 19–26. https://doi.org/10.1080/07303084.2020.1838362
Dyson, B., & Sutherland, S. (2015). Adventure education in your physical education program. In J. Lund & D. Tannehill (Eds.), *Standard-based physical education curriculum development* (pp. 229–254). Jones and Bartlett.
Ennis, C.D. (2015). Knowledge, transfer, and innovation in physical literacy curricula. *Journal of Sport and Health Science, 4*(2), 119–124. https://doi.org/10.1016/j.jshs.2015.03.001
Hämäläinen, J. (2012). Social pedagogical eyes in the midst of diverse understandings, conceptualisations and activities. *The International Journal of Social Pedagogy, 1*(1), 3–16. https://doi.org/10.14324/111.444.ijsp.2012.v1.1.002
Haneishi, K., Block, B., Zarco, E.P., Prados-Megías, M.E., & Johnson, M. (2023a). The Thirdspace movement model for inclusion and social justice in physical education. *JOPERD: The Journal of Physical Education, Recreation & Dance, 94*(4), 41–50. https://doi.org/10.1080/07303084.2023.2172111
Haneishi, K., Tse Sheng, T., Nkala, B., & Boyd, K. (2023b). Promoting Justice, Equity, Diversity, and Inclusion (JEDI) through a Game-Based Approach (GBA) in Physical Education. In S. Pill, E.A. Gambles & L. Griffin (Eds.), *Teaching games and sport for understanding*. 175–185, Routledge.
Hellison, D. (2011). *Teaching personal and social responsibility through physical activity* (3rd ed.). Human Kinetics.
Holt/Hale, S. (2015). The skill theme approach to physical education. In J. Lund & D. Tannehill (Eds.), *Standard-based physical education curriculum development* (pp. 205–228). Jones and Bartlett.
Lynch, S., Walton-Fisette, J. L., & Luguetti, C. (2021). *Pedagogies of social justice in physical education and youth sport*. Routledge.
Metzler, M., & Colquitt, G. (2021). *Instructional models for physical education* (4th ed.). Routledge.
Mitchell, S.A., Oslin, J., & Griffin, L.L. (2021). *Teaching sport concepts and skills: A tactical games approach* (4th ed.). Human Kinetics.
Mitchell, S.A., & Walton-Fisette, J.L. (2022). *The essentials of teaching physical education: Curriculum, instruction, and assessment*. Human Kinetics.
Moss, P. (2007). Starting strong: An exercise in international learning. *International Journal of Childcare and Education Policy, 1*(1), 11–21. https://doi.org/10.1007/2288-6729-1-1-11
O'Sullivan, M., Kinchin, G., & Enright, E. (2015). Cultural studies curriculum in physical activity and sport. In J. Lund & D. Tannehill (Eds.), *Standard-based physical education curriculum development* (3rd ed.) (pp. 337–364). Jones and Bartlett.
Rothuizen, J.J., & Harbo, L.J. (2017). Social pedagogy: An approach without fixed recipes. *International Journal of Social Pedagogy, 6*(1), 6–28. https://doi.org/0.14324/111.444.ijsp.2017.v6.1.002
Siedentop, D., Hastie, P., & van der Mars, H. (2020). *Complete guide to sport education* (3rd ed.). Human Kinetics.

Suggestions of Additional Resources

Butler, J. (2016). *Playing fair: Using student-invented games to prevent bullying, teach democracy, and promote social justice*. Human Kinetics.

Haneishi, K., Tse Sheng, T., Nkala, B., & Boyd, K. (2023). Promoting justice, equity, diversity, and inclusion (JEDI) through a game-based approach (GBA) in physical education. In S. Pill, E.A. Gambles & L. Griffin (Eds.), *Teaching games and sport for understanding*. Routledge.

8 Social Pedagogy and Social Justice Promotion in and through Physical Education

Fernando Santos, Tarkington Newman, María Fernández-Villarino and Jill Kochanek

Learning Objectives

At the end of this chapter, you will be able to:

- Operationalise social pedagogy through the concept of social justice life skills;
- Envision potential strategies to foster social justice life skills within Physical Education programming;
- Identify practitioners' roles and responsibilities in infusing a social justice life skill focus.

VIGNETTE

A Physical Education teacher has brought their group into a huddle at the end of the lesson to debrief key takeaways. During this conversation, another teacher walks toward their group, talking with a colleague. They make a derogatory racial remark (use the N*word) within earshot of the huddle. The Physical Education teacher hears this remark and continues with the dialogue, with an awareness that some youth may have also heard this remark. Rather than ignore these comments or assume that the youth did not hear them, the Physical Education teacher uses this situation as a teachable moment to promote an inclusive environment and social justice life skills among youth.

First, the Physical Education teacher privately calls in their peers and calls out the behaviour – identifying the harmful effects of the remarks and the need for adult leaders and educators to set a better example. At the beginning of the next lesson, he/she directly addresses the moment, explaining that such language would not be tolerated in their learning environment. They create space for youth to dialogue about what it means to be a colleague and leader who takes action to make everyone feel included and valued rather than othered or excluded. The Physical Education teacher assists youth in coming up with actions that they can take to embrace the diversity within the class rather than reinforce views that everyone is the same (be like a "family"). Instead, the class is a "community" with diverse backgrounds, experiences, skill sets, strengths and needs that everyone must honour for them to thrive and perform their best.

Introduction

In this chapter, we focus on the following social pedagogy tenets that have several implications for physical educators: (a) developing pedagogical approaches that place youth's needs at the centre-stage of Physical Education and sport programming; and (b) subsequently, moving beyond normative approaches that seek productivity, motivation (in the form of domestication), and obedience/control. This will be achieved by presenting the concept of *social justice life skills* and its potential applications (Box 8.1). These avenues for social pedagogy application can help consider political extremism, racism, and gender inequities and use Physical Education and sport to educate youth better to face these issues. The social pedagogy framework acknowledges the importance of helping youth create a sense of community and understand how to contribute to a better world through meaningful relationships with others. As stated in the opening vignette, the class is a "community" within which everyone must honoured for their differences and potential to thrive and perform their best. Therefore, to deconstruct inequities and foster social inclusion, social justice life skills can become tangible and actionable content for Physical Education teachers and youth sports coaches. Ultimately, by leveraging school Physical Education and sport as learning contexts, youth – the future of any society – are better positioned to become agents of change.

Box 8.1 Operationalising social justice life skills

- Social justice life skills are taught in ways that foster equity, diversity, and inclusion.
- Social justice life skills are more than mere skills but reflect attitudes, values, and worldviews.

For this reason, we advance the proposal of Camiré et al. (2022), which advocates for teaching youth life skills in ways beyond normative pedagogical approaches. Normative life skills teaching may consist of providing youth with opportunities to lead a group, ensuring all students/athletes engage with the proposed tasks, and peer debriefing about the leader's productivity within a task proposed by a Physical Education teacher. Normative life skills can risk reinforcing the notion that sport is a field where everyone is equal. Such a perspective, however, may decontextualise and disenfranchise the voices and experiences of many youth.

Box 8.2 Illustrative case studies

Normative approaches to development

- John is a student who is intrinsically motivated for Physical Education, enthusiastic about sport and able to engage, respect and lead others. However, John does so with disregard for diversity and without critical thinking. That is, John is leading in an identity-blind way that overlooks how others' diversity might meaningfully contribute to the collective goal and also how certain individuals may need additional support (to meet their needs given inequities relative to him given his identities and social privileges).

Transformative approaches to development

- Maria showcases most of John's attributes and skills. Nonetheless, Maria has learned skills to create an inclusive environment in Physical Education, promote the value of differences and critically question taken for granted assumptions (e.g., other students' problems are not mine to solve). Further, Maria has been able to transfer these skills to other life domains and is leading efforts to create awareness in the community about transgender athletes' rights.

Within Physical Education and sport settings, hegemonic and toxic masculinity are often viewed favourably. One example of hegemonic and toxic masculinity might be one person taking charge and being the loudest without allowing others to share their perspective, have a voice or make a meaningful contribution. Such views limit the conception of effective leadership and may disenfranchise and silence girls/females and gender-expansive youth. Thus, if a young person learns to lead by giving little consideration to how his/her biases may shape their actions, his/her behaviours/decisions may

Social Pedagogy and Social Justice Promotion 107

risk having harmful effects and reinforcing social inequities/injustices. This is why Camiré et al. (2022) provide insights about the need to teach youth life skills through strategies that go beyond a mere utilitarian approach (see Box 8.2) towards a *transformative teaching approach* focused on social justice life skills development.

Aligned with social pedagogy lenses, a transformative teaching approach may include strategies such as creating opportunities for youth to lead a group of students with the explicit objective of ensuring inclusion by challenging social inequities through antiracism practices, LGBTQ+ allyship, healthy masculinity and mental health literacy (see Box 8.2). Strategies such as peer debriefing and ensuring inclusion, voices, and choices for all are needed both in and outside Physical Education. Fostering social justice life skills requires Physical Education teachers, parents, and Physical Education Teacher Education (PETE) facilitators to pose broader questions than '*What should I teach and how?*'. Instead, they should be challenged to understand power imbalances and forces of oppression (i.e., cultural humility); develop concrete strategies to foster social justice life skills (i.e., cultural competence); and continuously reflect and engage with practice and theory (i.e., critical consciousness).

Until today, despite the need for social justice promotion within Physical Education and sport settings, most youth-centred programmes have focused on developing normative skills (Adamson et al., 2022). Social justice promotion and programming require all engaged stakeholders to take responsibility for the processes and outcomes connected to youth development. If social justice life skills simply became an add-on and a temporary pursuit, such programmes will fall short of making the on-going commitment necessary to facilitate wholescale skills development and transference Therefore, it is paramount to understand the processes and mechanisms connected to the teaching of social justice life skills. For this purpose, within the present chapter, we move beyond the work of Camiré et al. (2022) and propose a continuum to guide practitioners in their pedagogical efforts to infuse social justice life skills in and through Physical Education (see Figure 8.1. for an overview of the continuum).

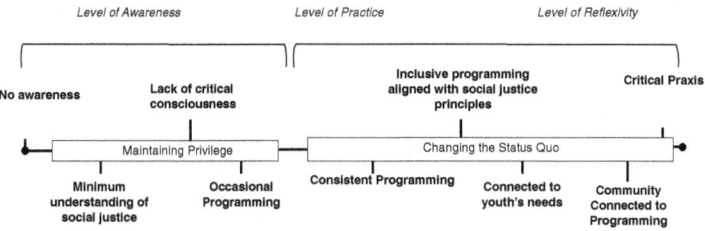

Figure 8.1 Social justice life skill programming continuum.

The continuum consists of three levels of engagement with social justice life skills programming. **At the first level (i.e., level of awareness)** Physical Education teachers, parents and PETE facilitators are not conscious of inequities, either in their context or more broadly throughout society and adopt narrow conceptualisations of social justice. At this level, they either use indirect (i.e., nondeliberate) strategies related to social justice promotion or prefer to teach it as an add-on to programming. In some cases, they may encounter social justice life skills as a problematic and unnecessary objective due to a need to maintain the status quo (Box 8.3). Within this level, strategies such as teaching leadership for youth to become more productive and achieve better results may be conducive to pedagogical mechanisms and processes that help maintain the status quo.

Box 8.3   Operationalisation

Physical Education teachers resort to pedagogical approaches that include appropriate sport skill development opportunities within a caring and autonomy-based climate. However, such a teaching approach does not include a focus on social justice life skills and deliberate efforts to foster social justice in and outside class.

At the second level (i.e., practice), practitioners' efforts are centred on promoting social justice and may include the systematic use of strategies in and outside class. Pedagogical decisions are determined by youths' developmental needs and the community's socio-political or cultural surroundings. For example, youth who hold 'privileged' social identities (e.g., cisgender, white male from an economically advantaged household) – because of their unique lived experiences – may be unaware of how their social identity affords them with social advantages (e.g., patriarchal systems). As a result, they may be less aware of how various forms of social identity oppression operate (i.e., at individual, institutional, and systemic levels). Personal-to-institutional and awareness-to-action sequencing can be a helpful pedagogical approach to scaffold challenges. Such an approach would entail building a young person's awareness of individual and institutional forms of oppression before fostering their capacity to act.

Box 8.4   Operationalisation

Physical Education teachers understand the characteristics of the community where the programme is being delivered and can deliberately

> target social justice life skills that align with youth's developmental needs in each lesson. Inclusive leadership may be taught to help others equitably achieve performance outcomes and serve to make a difference in and outside sport. This may include using leadership skills to problem-solve social justice issues associated with gender, ethnic background, and diverse performance levels, as well as understanding the importance of leadership in caring for others. Further, Physical Education teachers may engage parents and other community members to facilitate the transfer of social justice life skills to other life domains beyond Physical Education and sport.

While having critical awareness is necessary for action, an individual might not have personal awareness and be able to act in their interpersonal relationships. Institutional change might not occur until there is an understanding of institutional and systemic levels of oppression. Thus, action needs to be taken to raise awareness and change interpersonal dynamics, which does not necessarily require institutional-level awareness. Although youth-centred, this level of programming implies a systems-level approach that includes multiple decision-makers such as Physical Education teachers, parents, PETE facilitators and community members (Box 8.4). That is because social justice as a content and an outcome of programming needs to be openly, critically discussed, and positioned to ensure youth can face current social challenges and disrupt the status quo.

Finally, the **third level (i.e., level of reflexivity)** is associated with the need to create a sense of programme sustainability through continuous alignment between theory, practice and reflection (i.e., praxis). It becomes paramount for physical educators working with a social pedagogy perspective to connect to theory through research-to-practice partnerships, among other strategies, and reflect on how social justice life skills are indeed becoming processes and outcomes of programming. For instance, research-to-practice partnerships may involve the development of practice-based evidence to help solve real-world issues, whereas researchers, physical educators and social pedagogues forge meaningful relationships (Box 8.5). Failing to meet the requirements of a true praxis within programming may create fluctuations across levels and may do more harm than good, especially when programmes create false expectations to youth and community members. In this case, youth might make some progress along the continuum (i.e., raised awareness), but only experience changes in critical awareness with no substantial impacts on critical action.

> **Box 8.5 Operationalisation**
>
> Physical Education teachers and social pedagogues proactively understand the importance of assessing and reorganising programmatic efforts by providing voices to all actors, including youth, through creating social justice-oriented communities of practice. Reflection and reflexive practice may also involve support from polytechnic institutions and universities in programme evaluation.

The diverse levels included in this continuum are not mutually exclusive, as programmes can move across the continuum throughout time. For example, a Physical Education programme can have a social justice focus and, due to changes in funding and policy, subsequently shift away from such initiatives. Nonetheless, as schools move towards the more explicit component of the continuum, multiple strategies can be implemented to induce developmental redundancy (i.e., infusing social justice promotion efforts across domains). Based on what is described in the opening vignette, Physical Education teachers need to use situations within their classrooms as teachable moments to promote an inclusive environment and social justice life skills among youth.

Implications for Physical Education Teachers, Parents and PETE Facilitators

To further operationalise the proposed continuum, anti-oppressive practice (Sakamoto & Pitner, 2005) can be used as the guiding framework to provide strategies for various actors and guide Physical Education programming. Anti-oppressive practice is a theory-based resource that provides guidelines for applied efforts towards social justice. For this reason, it can serve as a framework for physical educators motivated to infuse social justice life skills into their programming. Below, we highlight three fundamental principles (Box 8.6) that physical educators need to adopt when working with anti-oppressive practice:

a. cultural competence
b. cultural humility, and
c. critical consciousness

These three key principles can help physical educators become more deliberate towards infusing social justice life skills into their programming and thus can contribute to helping youth foster social justice life skills as part of social pedagogy practice.

Box 8.6 Key definitions

a *Cultural competence* is associated with efforts to strive for social justice in culturally appropriate ways. Cultural competence regards the awareness, knowledge, and skills to engage in culturally sensitive ways with diverse individuals to promote their thriving and social justice.

b *Cultural humility* refers to understanding context, listening, and reflecting on power imbalances and structures to challenge them. Cultural humility requires understanding that learning is on-going given the limitations of our social identities/experiences and often done through mistakes. It's ultimately about recognising that one can never be truly culturally competent.

c *Critical consciousness* is the process of developing a critical praxis and reflecting on novel and adequate ways to teach and foster meaningful learning. Meaningful learning equates to efforts that challenge the status quo. Efforts to challenge social inequities are made in/through but not limited to pedagogy that helps youth engage in their critical consciousness-raising.

Cultural Competence

Social justice life skills' development can support youth's understanding and embracement of diversity (e.g., cultural, and other identity characteristics) for all to feel a sense of belonging and care. It is important to note that efforts to promote social justice life skills go beyond cultural competence, such as simply promoting diversity and inclusion, towards encouraging critical action that address social inequities. From a social justice perspective, caring for others should be enacted from a 'treat others as they want to be treated' and not 'treat others as you would want to be treated' perspective. This aligns with an approach that prioritises equity over equality. In this vein, leadership, as a social justice life skill, needs to be understood/taught from a non-dominant (critical and inclusive) view.

A non-dominant view of leadership suggests that leadership is action (to address a social issue or cause) that anyone can take regardless of their formal role or position. A non-dominant view of leadership also recognises that anyone has the capacity to develop leadership skills. Thus, leadership roles/responsibilities can be shared more widely rather than hierarchically limited to a few. A non-dominant perspective of leadership also deconstructs how leadership behaviours/attributes are defined according to a white, cisgender masculine, heteronormative status quo. This alternative leadership approach celebrates behaviours/attributes that share power with others via collaboration (*power with*) and inspire critical action to challenge inequities (*power to*). In addition, it is important to consider how views of leadership effectiveness are impacted by social identity biases and a leader's own experience. For example, women may experience a double bind when being assertive as a leader because that undermines their femininity. Black, Indigenous, and/or women of colour are culturally stereotyped as caretakers and leadership actions that show empathy, care, and support may be viewed as less laudable because it's what is socially expected relative to a white male that exhibits these actions and is seen as exceptional.

Thus, to move towards practice and reflection (i.e., the explicit and direct levels of the continuum), practitioners' efforts may need to be centred on making social justice life skills the contents for Physical Education and each class; positioning social justice life skills as an act of caring for others; resorting to youth-led and/or youth-centric approaches; and understanding activism as an important endeavour for youth development.

Cultural Humility

Before being tempted to develop strategies and activities for social justice life skills development, practitioners can reflect on the following questions:

- What are the dominant ways of thinking in the school and community?
- What are the main social challenges youth face in the school and community?
- To what extent physical educators afford privilege, and what are the possible experiences/areas where they lack knowledge or may have blind spots (i.e., social identity biases)?
- What voices are not heard?
- What strategies, if any, have been taken to foster social justice?
- What anti-oppressive actions have been taken?
- How, if at all, have current actions been effective in addressing inequities? And, in what ways could these actions be improved?

Based on the context and the answers to the questions above, efforts may need to be deployed towards understanding how current programmatic efforts are aligned with the levels presented in the continuum in Figure 8.1. This is particularly relevant because different practitioners may have diverse experience, preconceptions and beliefs, requiring significant time and effort to reach the last level of the continuum. Below, we present a progression of guiding principles with which Physical Education teachers (Box 8.7), parents (Box 8.8) and PETE facilitators (Box 8.9) could work in their effort to teach social justice life skills by moving across the continuum of curriculum programming.

Box 8.7 Progression for Physical Education teachers

- Define leadership as the social justice life skill to be developed in a lesson.
- Create activities to develop this social justice life skill (e.g., define leaders for each team and help them create rules that enable everyone to be included; create a mentorship programme where leaders will help a colleague for a whole year and thrive for a social justice cause).
- Assess this objective.
- Highlight how social justice life skills are relational and require caring for others.
- Place youth at the centre-stage of programming by giving them autonomy, voice, choice, and ownership – youth-led and/or youth-centric.
- Openly discuss social justice issues and create opportunities for youth to defend social justice causes (e.g., environment, LGBTQ+ rights), help community members who face injustices and use their agency to take political stands.

Box 8.8 Progression for parents

- Emphasise the importance of leadership outside school.
- Create opportunities for youth to practice social justice life skills (e.g., enable youth to help at a community centre or engage in a social justice cause).
- Assess objectives with the help of teachers and school staff.
- Openly discuss social justice issues with youth and other social pedagogues.
- Continuously reflect with the teachers and school staff.

Box 8.9 Progression for PETE facilitators

- Explicitly introduce social justice as a key content of quality Physical Education programming.
- Use the continuum to prompt self-assessment and reflection.

- Based on the participants' conceptualisations, create awareness about the need to adhere to strategies that connect to the practice and reflection components of the continuum.
- Discuss potential strategies that can be applied by each participant.
- Infuse social justice life skills across the entire PETE programme in modules such as pedagogy, didactics, and professional identity, among many others.
- Assess the participant's ability to understand and fulfil the continuum's proposed objectives and pedagogical principles.

In light of these guiding principles, Physical Education programmes should also take into account the need to avoid weaponising social justice life skills – claiming a social justice mandate to oblige politically correct discourses without any appropriate processes to achieve this endeavour.

To achieve such a premise, it is important for practitioners who work under a social pedagogy perspective to bear in mind that:

- Learning social justice life skills may not be a direct result of learner-centred pedagogies;
- Learning social justice life skills requires direct and explicit strategies;
- Learning social justice life skills implies engagement with the social world that involves teachers, parents, and other pedagogues.

Critical Consciousness

Physical Education teachers, parents and PETE facilitators need to develop critical consciousness to engage with social justice and social justice life skills as part of their effort to impact youth's learning outcomes. Critical consciousness can help educators and pedagogues to use the continuum appropriately. Thus, we propose that professionals who seek to develop youth's social justice life skills need to:

- Extend the principles associated with normative pedagogical models, since these have a neutral effect on social justice;
- Create meaningful bonds with community members and provide them with voices beyond a mere artificial engagement with context and community;
- Connect with theory by coming together with researchers (and vice-versa) and alternative theoretical proposals;
- Recognise everyone's roles and responsibilities in knowledge production (i.e., all knowledge is relevant).

Although these are essential needs for practitioners, they are undoubtedly challenging to address within the context of school Physical Education and after-school sports for many reasons. First, practitioners may have been trained and socialised to think normatively and assume that their efforts generate positive outcomes – without this being always the case. Second, engaging with theory to reimagine practice requires cultural humility, competence, time, and effort. Third, modern societies reinforce the need to achieve tasks that result in profit, and social justice life skills might not be an organisational priority. Thus, sustained efforts centred on social justice life skills, and a coherent critical praxis require a solid commitment to youth development and societal change.

Advice from the Field

What are the benefits of implementing a social pedagogy approach to Physical Education? Dwyane (USA, high school coach): As a Black male from a more impoverished background to be there, I'm kind of, I'm not saying I'm the first Black person they've probably met, right; but I might be one of their first experiences one-on-one with a Black male. And just based on certain things we read about, or we see, I can be very intimidating just on how I look. I can be a more intimidating person to interact with, especially based on that I coach girls as well, right? ... But I always feel like it's my responsibility to make sure that, in that, I'm being authentic in who I am, but I'm also showing them that you can't really judge a book by its cover.

Key Points

- Social justice promotion is attainable and can be fostered across Physical Education and sport;
- Teachers and other social pedagogues can and should infuse cultural humility, cultural competence and critical consciousness principles in their practice;
- Social justice life skills and transformative teaching approaches can move the needle towards social justice promotion;
- Applied efforts should consider cultural, political and social influences on youth and youth development.

Summary

Throughout this chapter, we have focused on providing strategies that promote the development of social justice life skills in and through Physical

Education. Through the tenets of social pedagogy, we seek to place the needs of students at the centre of programming. The strategies aimed at Physical Education teachers, parents and PETE facilitators are situated in three diverse levels as part of a dynamic continuum:

i Level of awareness;
ii Level of practice;
iii Level of reflexivity.

Within these levels, it is important for teachers to create space for youth to dialogue about what it means to be a colleague and leader who acts (see opening vignette). Overall, the purpose of implementing and developing these strategies is to ensure inclusion, challenge social inequities, and provide opportunities for young people to express themselves and positively contribute to a better society.

Reflection Questions and Activities

- In what ways, if any, do you currently model or exercise cultural humility, cultural competence and/or critical consciousness in your work with youth?
- How can you build off what you currently do to help youth engage in these processes themselves?
- How, if at all, can you engage youth to share their experiences with inclusion and exclusion (or a moment where they felt a sense of belonging or lack thereof) in a movement setting within a current activity or lesson that you do?
- From this reflection and dialogue, in what ways might you emphasise the importance of creating an inclusive environment for all to succeed and thrive rather than reinforce false notions of a level playing field (i.e., hard work yields success)?

References

Adamson, B., Adamson, M., Clarke, C., Richardson, E., & Sydnor, S. (2022). Social justice through sport and exercise studies: A manifesto. *Journal of Sport and Social Issues*, *46*(5), 407–444. https://doi.org/10.1177/01937235221099150

Camiré, M., Newman, T., Bean, C., & Strachan, L. (2022). Reimagining positive youth development and life skills in sport through a social justice lens. *Journal of Applied Sport Psychology*, *34*(6), 1058–1076. https://doi.org/10.1080/10413200.2021.1958954

Sakamoto, I., & Pitner, R. (2005). Use of critical consciousness in anti-oppressive social work practice: Disentangling power dynamics at personal and structural levels. *The British Journal of Social Work*, *35*(4), 435–452. https://doi.org/10.1093/bjsw/bch190

Suggestions of Additional Resources

Educational resources from RISE: https://risetowin.org/take-action/index.html#resources

Kaplowitz, D.R., Griffin S.R., & Seyka, S. (2019). *Race dialogues: A facilitator's guide to tackling the elephant in the classroom*. Teachers College Press.

Kochanek, J., Secaras, L., & Erickson, K. (2022). Dialogue in Athletics: An evaluation of a social justice education program in high school sports. *Journal of Applied Sport Psychology*. Advance online publication. https://doi.org/10.1080/10413200.2022.2084181

Part IV

Assessment in and of Physical Education Programs Developed According to Social Pedagogy

9 Social Pedagogy and Assessment in Physical Education

Incorporating Students within Assessment Approaches

Shrehan Lynch and Jennifer Norley

Learning Objectives

By the end of this chapter, we hope that you will have an understanding why social assessment is essential in Physical Education and we provide an example to help you understand it further and potentially apply it within your context in the future. At the end of this chapter, you will be able to:

- Know what a social pedagogy-oriented assessment model looks like in Physical Education.
- Understand what domains of learning are considered as social pedagogy in Physical Education.
- Apply the social pedagogy assessment method demonstrated to your context and change your assessment procedures as needed.

VIGNETTE

Imagine you are a Physical Education student completing a basketball unit. You don't present the "typical" phenotype that would socially identify you as "athletic", nor have you ever had a great interest in Physical Education. However, you have other attributes that you feel are unique and that make you who you are. Now, you have just been told that in the final assessment, you will need to complete the beep/beep test and potentially other fitness-related tests (e.g., Cooper run, sit-up test, etc.). However, you have not practised such tasks during the unit. You couldn't work out specific fitness content during that Physical Education unit. You're shocked, you don't understand why you are asked to perform these tasks that are not familiar to you, and you feel pessimistic about partaking in the final assessment. You will be put off attending Physical Education in the future.

Likely, the reasons for these feelings include the assessment focusing on the physical domain while you have so much more to showcase your learning in basketball. You've positively related with your peers, helped some of them to perform basketball skills, and learned that when you put all you have into the task, a defeat in a basketball game is okay. You feel embarrassed and ashamed to complete the beep test in front of your peers, and you don't understand why the scores will be posted for everyone to see.

The above excerpt exemplifies one situation in Physical Education where the pedagogy and assessment do not meet social pedagogy educational tenets. They emphasise only the physical domain of learning. Such practice is dated and flawed within a 21st-century holistic approach to Physical Education, where teaching and learning need to occur in a democratic ethos.

Introduction

Society is structured in ways that each of us is complicit in systems of inequality. Thus, educators have a duty to practice socially just/transformative pedagogies that allow students opportunities to engage in their learning and active contribution to a fairer society (Sensoy & DiAngelo, 2017). When students are invited to contribute to their learning, teaching spaces are more democratic, which can create learning communities where students can learn social skills they use and apply in their daily lives (hooks, 1994). Social skills that students might employ are those such as actively speaking to others, deliberation, and negotiation (for more examples see Table 1.1, and the Diamond Model). Thus, socially informed pedagogy is extended both within and outside the school context, supporting young people beyond the scope of formal learning spaces.

Teaching, learning, assessment, context, and content are interlinking aspects of pedagogy that need to be considered when considering democratic teaching spaces (see Figure 9.1). Elements of the pedagogical sphere do not happen independently (e.g., assessment can't occur without teaching having taken place). However, interestingly, assessment could occur without learning (pre-assessment, for example). This idea that pedagogy is interrelated is a concrete aspect of social pedagogy and could be considered part of the 'Common Third' (see Table 1.1).

As part of the complexity of pedagogy, assessment itself is complex, highly political, and a social activity, which can have a transformative influence on Physical Education content, delivery, and orientation (Hay & Penney, 2012). Viewed this way, teaching spaces revolve around the idea that assessment is the fundamental place where teaching and learning are evaluated in an open, reciprocal, and conversational way (Parkison, 2018). Assessment needs could become

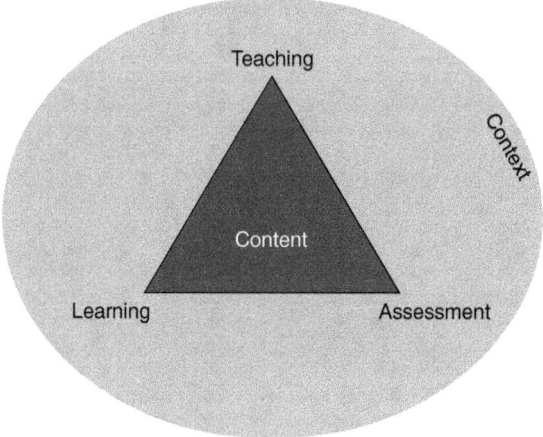

Figure 9.1 The interrelated complexity of pedagogy.

dialogical and attempt to engage students with democratic principles rooted in co-construction, ownership, and student voice (Lynch & Curtner-Smith, 2019). Consequently, we recommend that assessment is a highly social process that engages and informs students about their learning in Physical Education. In that way, students learn that assessment does not occur independently; it is part of a complex pedagogical action that includes learning, teaching, context, and content (see Figure 9.1). These pivotal assumptions give life to a social pedagogy approach to assessment in that it is highly participatory and part of the Common Third (see *CSP*[1]: **Participation & Preparing for Participation** in Table 1.1).

Many have theorised how Physical Education can have a more social approach to assessment, assessing more than physical learning. Andrew Frapwell, an English Physical Education consultant, commonly shares the 'Head, Heart, Hands' model, which has been adapted and reworked by many in the Physical Education community to suit their specific contexts. The premise of the model is that you assess in three broad areas: head (knowledge, understanding, rules, etc.), heart (confident, leadership, resilience, etc.), hands (physicality, fitness, technique, etc.). Similar to this well-known model, the 'Me in Physical Education' approach was born, a highly social assessment approach where students can see themselves within the subject and assessment itself. As the authors of this chapter, we are advocates of the 'Me in Physical Education' approach. Throughout the rest of the chapter, we explain why and demonstrate how we use this model in one of our schools as it links directly to a social pedagogical approach to Physical Education. As stated in the opening vignette, a social pedagogical approach can be more relevant than a 21st-century holistic approach to Physical Education, where teaching and learning need to occur in a democratic ethos.

Table 9.1 Assessment point in the 'Me in Physical Education' approach

Bronze	Silver	Gold	Platinum
(a) Analyst ME (CSP*: *Participation & Preparing for Participation*) - To respectfully but constructively evaluate performance to bring about impactful improvements			
I can analyse performance to identify a WWW** & EBI***	I can analyse performance to identify a more detailed WWW & EBI	I can analyse performance to identify at least two relevant WWWs & EBIs	I can analyse performance to identify three or more relevant WWWs & EBIs
I can decide on one way that either I or someone else can improve my/someone else's performance	I can decide on two ways that either I or someone else can improve my/someone else's performance	I can decide on several ways that either I or someone else can improve my/someone else's performance	I can decide on several ways to improve performance and can prioritise some clear targets to improve my/someone else's performance
I can utilise the feedback provided to improve one aspect of my performance	I can utilise the feedback provided to improve some aspects of my performance	I can utilise the feedback provided to improve many aspects of my performance	I can utilise the feedback provided to substantially improve most aspects of my performance
(b) Social ME (CSP*: *The Common Third* & CSP*: *Participation, Preparing for Participation*) – To demonstrate positive communication, leadership skills and teamwork within a Physical Education environment.			
On occasion, I can use my communication skills to offer some feedback to peers to increase/improve their attainment	I can use my communication skills to offer some feedback to peers to increase/improve their attainment	I can use my communication skills to offer constructive and pertinent feedback to peers to increase/improve their attainment	I can use my communication skills to offer constructive, relevant and focused feedback to peers to increase/improve their attainment
On occasion/with support, I can work cooperatively with others in lessons	I can work cooperatively with others in lessons most of the time	I can work cooperatively with others in lessons all the time	I can consistently work cooperatively with others in lessons and encourage others to follow my good example
		I can take a leading role within my group/team	I can take a leading role within my group/team by organising them and motivating them to succeed

(*Continued*)

Social Pedagogy and Assessment in Physical Education 125

Table 9.1 (Continued)

Bronze	Silver	Gold	Platinum
(c) Resilient ME (CSP*: *The Diamond Model: taking risks and learning, empowerment*) – To build the capacity to recover quickly from perceived threats and to learn how to push myself beyond a comfort zone.			
On occasion, I have the ability to overcome tough/challenging situations	I have the ability to overcome tough/challenging situations most of the time	I have the ability to overcome tough/challenging situations almost all of the time	I have the ability to overcome tough/challenging situations quickly
On occasion, I feel confident enough to take calculated risks in order to experience more success	I feel confident enough to take calculated risks in order to experience more success most of the time	I feel confident enough to take calculated risks in order to experience more success	I feel confident enough to take regular calculated risks in order to experience more success. I am always willing to try tasks/activities
I demonstrate mental toughness in some of the activities that we are covering in Physical Education	I demonstrate mental toughness in many of the activities that we are covering in Physical Education	I demonstrate mental toughness in almost all of the activities that we are covering in Physical Education	I consistently demonstrate mental toughness in all of the activities that we are covering in Physical Education
		On occasion, I can help others to overcome adversity in Physical Education	I regularly help others to overcome adversity in Physical Education
(d) Creative ME (CSP*: *Creativity: using imagination as co-production*) – To explore and experiment with new ideas and concepts in Physical Education			
On occasion, I can use a few simple but different ways to express & communicate ideas, solve problems and overcome challenges	I can use some simple but different ways to express & communicate ideas, solve problems and overcome challenges	I can use many imaginative ways to express & communicate ideas, solve problems and overcome challenges	I can consistently create and apply imaginative ways to express & communicate ideas, solve problems and overcome the more advanced challenges
On occasion, I will explore and experiment with some techniques/compositional ideas	I will explore and experiment with some techniques/compositional ideas to produce more effective outcomes	I will explore and experiment with many techniques/compositional ideas to produce more effective outcomes	I will explore and experiment with a wide variety of techniques/compositional ideas to produce more effective outcomes

(*Continued*)

Table 9.1 (Continued)

Bronze	Silver	Gold	Platinum
I will experience some success when experimenting with some basic tactics/formations/compositional ideas	I will experience a good level of success when experimenting with some tactics/formations/compositional ideas	I will experience a good level of success when experimenting with more complex tactics/formations/compositional ideas	I will experience a very high level of success when experimenting with more complex tactics/formations/compositional ideas

(e) Healthy ME (CSP*: *The Diamond Model: wellbeing & happiness***)** – To understand how safe exercise in a range of physical activities positively benefits my health, fitness and well-being

Bronze	Silver	Gold	Platinum
I can complete short periods of physical activity within an activity	I can complete longer bursts of physical activity within an activity	I can remain active for longer periods of time within an activity	I have a very good level of physical fitness to cope with the demands of all activities covered within Physical Education
I can recount some reasons as to why physical activity is important and is integral to me leading a more active lifestyle	I understand why physical activity is important and can lead others in a warm up/cool down.	I can describe the short term/long term effects of physical activity on the body and can identify some of the major muscles/bones	I can evaluate why physical activity is needed to lead a more healthy/active lifestyle and can use this information to support others to participate in more regular exercise
I regularly demonstrate at least one way to improve my health/well-being. E.g. I walk to/from school five days a week	I will attend at least one extra-curricular club inside/outside of school	I will attend at least two extra-curricular clubs inside/outside of school	I am a committed member of many extracurricular clubs/teams inside/outside of school
I am always dressed appropriately to ensure that I can take part in physical activity safely and follow the Sarah Bonnell Way at all times	I demonstrate fair play, respect and good sportspersonship to ensure there is a safe environment for everyone to participate in	I can support others to demonstrate fair play, respect and good sportspersonship to ensure there is a safe environment for everyone to participate in	I consistently embody the SB Way and act as an exemplary role model for others to emulate to ensure there is a safe environment for everyone to participate in.

(*Continued*)

Social Pedagogy and Assessment in Physical Education 127

Table 9.1 (Continued)

Bronze	Silver	Gold	Platinum
(f) Physical ME (CSP*: *The Diamond Model: Wellbeing & Happiness*) – To be able to develop, select and appropriately apply skills, tactics and/or compositional ideas in a range of sporting environments.			
I can demonstrate a skill/movement when assisted or through direct instruction	I can select and combine some core skills with control and accuracy	I can perform the more complex skills with control, accuracy and fluency	I can select, link and combine the more advanced skills/techniques in a range of situations with excellent control, accuracy and fluency
I can use the fundamental skills (e.g. running, jumping, hitting, etc.) for the activity in isolation and under competitive pressure.	I can demonstrate all of the fundamental skills and some core skills for the activity in isolation and under competitive pressure	I can demonstrate all of the core skills and some advanced skills for the activity in isolation and under competitive pressure	I can demonstrate all of the advanced skills for the activity in isolation and under competitive pressure
I can demonstrate some of the necessary fitness components during performance in a variety of contexts	I can show sufficient physical fitness to perform with some effectiveness	I can demonstrate good levels of physical fitness and psychological control to meet the demands of the activity(ies)	I can demonstrate excellent levels of physical fitness and psychological control to meet the demands of the activity(ies)
On occasion, I can show some tactical awareness within a game situation	I can show sufficient tactical awareness within a game situation	I can show good tactical awareness within a game situation. I have an influential effect in competitive situations	I can show excellent tactical awareness within a game situation. I have a highly influential effect in competitive situations

* Concept of Social Pedagogy (for more details see Table 1.1).
** *WWW* stands for *What Went Well*
*** *EBI* stands for *Even Better If*

Advice from the Field

Jennifer Norley (England, Head of Physical Education, Teacher, Author)

The National organisation for Physical Education in England named 'the Association for Physical Education' stated in 2014, that effective assessment in Physical Education needs to be supportive, engaging, and motivational to enable all students to become more competent, confident, creative, and reflective movers (CPS: Creativity, in Table 1.1). However, finding inclusive, purposeful, and rigorous assessment examples in Physical Education has been, at times, difficult for many Physical Education departments utilising procedures/processes that are traditional, outdated, trauma-inducing, confrontational and very often favour the more physically able. This statement is profoundly concerning, and mirrors concerns expressed by students I spoke with when I began my position as a Curriculum Leader in a Physical Education Department in East London. Students regularly voiced that the Physical Education department's assessment process (at the time) led them to feel unseen, unheard, low in confidence and "rubbish at Physical Education". I knew that something had to change for students to feel represented and set to work on a new, more inclusive assessment model that would still translate into the whole school context but would allow students to be rewarded for their ability to analyse performance(s), demonstrate resilience, experiment with ideas/concepts, showcase their creativity, exhibit the qualities of a 'good sportsperson', show their knowledge/understanding, as well as proving themselves to be more skilful/competent movers. With that in mind, I set about achieving the above goal in complete consultation with the stakeholders that really mattered – the students, the Physical Education staff, and the parents/carers.

> Griffin (2023) outlines that no matter what assessment methods we (as educators) choose to utilise, there is always an element of forcing round pegs into square holes and that we need to be solutions focussed to find a 'best fit' model.

In an attempt to find the best fit model for my specific context, the new assessment procedure needed to be more fit for purpose, inclusive, achievable and flexible. Initial thoughts needed to be prepped, planned, experimented with, adapted, and regularly updated. This needed to be viewed as a never-ending project continuously flexed and expanded through a perpetual evaluative process. It was deemed that a 'hybrid' assessment process would best suit our context. This is where students are assessed in their ability and demonstration of 'soft skills' – what we know as social skills, integral to everyday life and very much, to us, hard skills! In this way, the social aspect was essential, and we began a continued dialogue with our students through our assessment practices. We choose to assess our students in various ways, but mainly through a lesson-by-lesson worksheet where upon entry to the changing room, we give students learning question worksheets and allow them to self-assess themselves. Then, either throughout and/or at the end of the lessons, they can go back to that worksheet before submission and update it with their progress.

We have adopted the 'Me in Physical Education' approach and adjusted it to suit our context, it most heavily aligns to the Diamond Model and tenants of social pedagogy. We assess in six different areas, including: analysing, social, physical, resilience, creativity, and health. In Table 9.1, you will see an example of what each of the assessment points look like for a Year 7 and 8 student (aged 11–14). Of course, depending on your own context, your content would need revising. WWW stands for What Went Well and EBI stands for Even Better If as terminology within our documents. This is an overall macro assessment guide that can be used lesson to lesson to help inform learning, pedagogy, and content.

The assessment points are no secret to students, they are transparently displayed and open for negotiation. As you can see, they are also progressive, so students might begin at bronze and gradually move through to gold/platinum towards the end of the unit. We must make a note on the categorization 'bronze, silver, gold, platinum' these are merely personal achievement areas and do not correlate to any form of hierarchisation between or among students, they are personalized points and to the educator they are quite neutral and simply used to empower individual students to strive within the class to learn more. Moreover, they are not used as an independent assessment tool. At a micro lesson level, the macro assessment descriptors are used in combination, we provide an example of a lesson idea with social assessment used, see Table 9.2. The lesson question, success criteria and starter activity are all based on a student's ability to build the social or creative domain with a Physical Education setting. The first example is related to the 'social me' in athletics. The second focuses on the 'creative me' and is based on a dance lesson. The worksheets, which would be given to students at the beginning of the lesson clearly identify how the lesson focuses on many elements which are beyond the physical domain and contribute to a social pedagogical approach. We hope these examples show to you how the macro assessment is put into action on a lesson/lesson (micro) basis.

Table 9.2 Example of a worksheet given to students used in athletics and dance (edited for book)

Key stage 3 Athletics – relay lesson

Context: In an Athletics relay lesson (4 × 100m), the focus is on how well students can build and showcase their leadership skills while attempting to become more effective and efficient when changing the baton (improving their technique cooperatively as a team and trying to reduce their changeover time). Students will learn this through learning about the upsweep and downsweep baton changeover techniques through team coaches who has a resource that includes the information necessary for the techniques. The teacher is a facilitator of peer teaching.

'Social ME' learning question:	Keywords:
How can I demonstrate positive teamwork skills to ensure the baton is successfully exchanged?	1 Effective 2 Efficient 3 Teamwork

Success criteria: 'Social Me'

Competent	Proficient	Advanced	World Class
I will be able to demonstrate at least ONE of the five teamwork skills to help my team to experience four successful relay changeovers.	I will be able to demonstrate at least TWO of the five teamwork skills to help my team to experience three successful relay changeovers.	I will be able to demonstrate at least THREE of the five teamwork skills to help my team to experience three successful relay changeovers. I will make TWO suggestions for improvement.	I will be able to demonstrate at least ALL of the five teamwork skills to help my team experience three successful relay changeovers. I will make THREE suggestions for improvement.

Starter activity / DO NOW	1 These are the top five teamwork skills (that spell DICES) that will be required for success in today's relay changeover lesson. Can you rank them in order of importance? **D**ELEGATION – making sure that everyone is fully involved and has a clear job/role. **I**DEAS – offering/listening to suggestions to improve performance. **C**OMMUNICATION – being respectful, clear & concise with your language. **E**FFICIENCY – completing tasks as quickly & effectively as possible. **S**UPPORT – building each other up and remaining positive/reflective
Starter activity / DO NOW	2 Justify which ONE of the teamwork skills that you might find the most difficult and how you could overcome this within a team

Note: We will often complete a couple of progress checks to remind students of the lesson focus and to prevent them from straying back into the "I'm not very good at running, so I'm not doing well in this lesson" rhetoric.

(Continued)

Table 9.2 (Continued)

Key stage 3 Dance – dance based warm up

Context: This is the first in the sequence of a set of dance lessons, it is an introduction to warming up in dance and the lesson focus is getting students to be creative in creating a warmup of their own including their own movements. The teacher is a facilitator within this lesson and the students are given creative ownership.

'Creative ME' learning question:	**Keywords:**
How can I create a dance based warm up and what do I need to do in order to get my movements in time with the music?	1 Timing 2 Energy 3 Accuracy 4 Choreograph

Success criteria: 'Creative Me'

Competent	Proficient	Advanced	World Class
With help from my peers/the teacher, I will co-create a dance based warm up that includes at least five movements	I can make some suggestions to help create our group's dance based warm up that includes at least six movements.	I can make several, positive suggestions to help create our group's dance based warm up that includes at least seven movements.	I can lead my group to create a unique and advanced warm up that includes at least eight different pulse-raising movements.

Starter activity / DO NOW	Watch the video and answer the following questions: [insert a video of your choice appropriate for your context, the video highlights an aerobic dance warm up] 1 Create names for at least three moves on the video. 2 What do you think the hardest and easiest move is? Why? 3 How should you structure and aerobic warm up? 4 Create your own moves and add to the routine.
Warm up	Copy the aerobic warm up you just watched. Pay attention to the moves, timing, and repetitions.

Note: We will often complete a couple of progress checks to remind students of the lesson focus and remind students that dance is for everybody. Lots of students feel self-conscious in dance lessons so we make a point that they should be fun, and music should be culturally appropriate.

Summary and Key Points

Throughout Chapter 9, we explain the need for social pedagogy in Physical Education and what a social pedagogical approach looks like. We have demonstrated that different learning domains should be considered in a social pedagogical approach. And, we have highlighted the importance of recognising that assessment is part of a complex pedagogical process. It is hoped that the ideas in this chapter provoke thought for individuals wishing to implement a social approach to their assessment approaches and stimulate some ideas!

Reflection Questions and Activities

- Considering your own Physical Education course now, how do you assess your students? What do you assess? When do you assess? How much voice do students get within this process?
- Discuss with your colleagues within your department how to make your assessment processes more social, what could you implement from your reading that could be relevant?
- Set yourself as a department a couple of assessment goals, implement them and review them in a month.

Note

1 CSP stands for Concept of Social Pedagogy (see Chapter 1, Table 1.1).

References

Association for Physical Education, AfPE. (2014). Guidance on assessment: National Curriculum (2014). Available from: https://www.afpe.org.uk/physical-education/guidance-on-assessment/ [accessed 22 May 2023].

Griffin, B. (2023). Key Stage 3 PE: Choosing an assessment model that helps pupils thrive. Available from: https://resources.pupilprogress.com/choosing-assessment-model-ks3-pe [accessed 22 May 2023].

Hay, P., & Penney, D. (2012). *Assessment in physical education: A sociocultural perspective*. Routledge.

hooks, b. (1994). *Teaching to transgress*. Routledge.

Lynch, S., & Curtner-Smith, M. (2019). 'You have to find your slant, your groove': One physical education teacher's efforts to employ transformative pedagogy. *Physical Education and Sport Pedagogy, 24*(4), 359–372. https://doi.org/10.1080/17408989.2019.1592146

Parkison, P. (2018). Assessment as dialogue: Reframing assessment. *Curriculum & Teaching Dialogue, 20*(1/2), 89–179. Retrieved from: https://www.infoagepub.com/products/Curriculum-and-Teaching-Dialogue-Vol-20

Sensoy, O., & DiAngelo, R. (2017). *Is everyone really equal? An introduction to key concepts in social justice education*. Teachers College Press.

Suggestions of Additional Resources

1 Pedagogies of Social Justice in Physical Education and Youth Sport Book: https://www.routledge.com/Pedagogies-of-Social-Justice-in-Phyical-Education-and-Youth-Sport/Lynch-Walton-Fisette-Luguetti/p/book/9780367755348
2 Socially Just Physical Education & Youth Sport Website: https://sociallyjustphysicaleducationandyouthsport.wordpress.com/
3 Lynch, S., & Monk, H. (2017). The A-Z of assessment. *Physical Education Matters*, *12*(1), 13–15. https://repository.uel.ac.uk/item/86vyz

10 Digitally Supported Assessment in Physical Education with a Social Pedagogy Perspective

Allyson Carvalho de Araújo, Alison Pereira Batista and Márcio Romeu Ribas de Oliveira

Learning Objectives

At the end of this chapter, you will be able to:

- Identify the potential of using interaction and collaboration as principles to articulate assessment with the digital technology universe.
- Plan and propose teaching and assessment processes through the use of digital language based on dialogue and collaboration.

VIGNETTE

A Physical Education teacher has been working in high school for 25 years. While walking through the corridors, he overhears a group of students criticising his teaching methodology, especially his assessment practices. Thus, he decides to participate in that dialogue. The students were surprised and interrupted the conversation, but the teacher insisted they continue and promised to listen to them without reacting negatively. After listening to them carefully, the teacher admitted that students' opinions impacted him and highlighted that he reproduced what his teachers had done. He acknowledged the need for self-improvement and committed to meeting the demands. Facing this scenario, the teacher asked the following questions in the subsequent class: What topics would you like to work on? How would you want to be assessed? After a debate of ideas and a democratic voting process, the students suggested including transgender athletes in sports competitions. They also voted for producing content on digital platforms as assessment tools for the teaching unit. The challenges will be enormous because the teacher has a history of reproducing and applying traditional assessment instruments (exams, seminars, written assessments, among others). Moreover, he must follow the whole learning process and not just observe only the final products. In this chapter, we raise the following driving question to help the teacher reflect on his assessment practices: How can a teacher plan, implement, and evaluate instruction using digitally supported and formative assessment?

Introduction

Assessment is considered one of the most complicated and controversial teaching elements that Physical Education teachers deal with daily. For at least 50 years, education systems worldwide have sought to activate and develop the topic of assessment in Physical Education. In the last three decades, the literature points out that a traditional assessment perspective is established and linked to physical fitness tests or subjective assessment forms, such as assessing students' effort, participation, and clothing (López-Pastor et al., 2013). In a new review of what was produced and reported in the literature on assessment in Physical Education, Moura and collaborators (2020) state that Physical Education teachers continue to use assessment only to classify students. In the scenario presented in the vignette, students do not seem to adequately understand the meaning of assessment in Physical Education and distance themselves from teachers. Given their stance, it becomes challenging for the teacher to align the assessment topic with social pedagogy assumptions, considering that traditional forms of assessment focus on knowledge efficiency, equating this with goals to be achieved based on standardised learning objectives.

In a different move, we invite you to think about assessment from a perspective other than measuring students' learning and classification on an objective scale. Considering learning as an act of social significance based on experienced or studied topics, assessment must also be understood as a process of collective discovery and synthesis of perspectives on the world. This way of thinking aligns with what has been called a formative (centred on the process and not the goal) and shared (among all subjects involved in the process) assessment and demands a review of our practices as teachers concerning the reason for our pedagogical actions to promote greater engagement and decision-making on the part of the students (López-Pastor et al., 2022).

In this sense, assessing involves teachers listening and being aware of the student's ways of knowing (Certeau, 2014). By paying attention to what the student declares, the teacher can have the desired learning objectives on the horizon. However, they must also condition their students' opinions regarding those objectives. Otherwise, they will not understand the wealth of potential that all students present when assimilating or finding new knowledge. Considering education as a cultural learning process, we expect each new perception of Physical Education topics to be influenced by social, political, environmental, ethical, aesthetic, and emotional elements. This process produces many forms of learning expressions in numerous languages.

To be faithful to a formative and shared assessment, we need to silence what we know about assessment but remember our professional learning. The teacher in the vignette felt eager to hear what students were discussing regarding their assessment. When mediating his listening with what the students had to say about their needs and desires, the teacher opened a path to understanding: assessing what is learned and taught needs to be a daily exercise. The teacher started incorporating a collegial and dialogic mindset concerning assessment practices by listening to what was being discussed.

That is why, in this chapter, we seek to update the understanding of assessment as a reflective move of the teacher who seeks to understand how students activate the knowledge discussed in meetings/classes with their reading of the world. Under such a perspective, the teacher does not seek to classify or hierarchise students but instead integrates student, teacher, and social knowledge to expand the forms of student understanding that will be assessed. The basis of thought that inspires us to think about assessment in these terms comes from Freirean pedagogy (Freire, 1998a; 1998b; 2000), in which the ideas of collective autonomy and reflective pedagogical practice are foundational for education and for any form of understanding (words, gestures, content) of the world (Freire, 1998b).

Reviewing the Communication Process in Assessment: The Role of Technologies

In a period of rapid information and communication spread that sometimes does not favour us in a critical, thoughtful reading of the world, it seems interesting to think of assessment as a communication process that contributes to our growth and learning. We share the idea that the teaching environment is, par excellence, a communicative space, given that there is no way to learn and teach if we do not communicate (Freire, 1987). Traditionally, as reported in the previous paragraphs, assessment processes have been based on a linear model of communication in which the sender (teacher) and the receiver (student) play defined roles with little interaction. In this mode of communication, the message is previously defined and unilaterally examined. Collaborative and evaluative teaching and learning processes presuppose a less linear and hierarchical relationship between subjects who simultaneously are senders and receivers. This is why we consider it essential to highlight some ideas, such as the *prosumer* concept, and relate them to the concepts of social pedagogy presented in Chapter 1 (see Table 1.1).

At a time when we have a vast range of ways to inform/communicate on the Internet, each access to the Web connects us to a network in which machines and humans act as agents that can only transmit or even re-signify

Digitally Supported Assessment in Physical Education   137

Table 10.1 The prosumer concept and its relation to concepts of social pedagogy

Concept	Explanation	Relation to concepts of social pedagogy
Prosumer	The concept reflects a shift towards a more participatory and interactive model, where individuals are not just consumers of products or information, but actively contribute to the production process. This concept has been fuelled by technological advancements that empower individuals to both create and consume in various domains.	Considering both teachers and students as prosumers aligns with the idea of full **Participation** (*CSP**), as a need to be part of all social construction processes, and the idea of **Creativity** (*CSP**), as the possibility to avoid linear approaches to problem-solving. In this sense, the **Common Third** concept (*CSP**) is addressed as a concept to strengthen relationships between the teacher and the students and weaken power hierarchies.

*Concept of Social Pedagogy (for more details, see Table 1.1).

messages in this multi-user environment. This network has no limit to the connections of meanings and agents. The idea of having *prosumers* (see Table 10.1) (García-Galera & Valdivia, 2014; Toffler, 2022) in communication means enabling more fruitful possibilities for thinking about assessment as a process in which teachers and students are interlocutors of complementary perceptions on the teaching topic. With collaboration and interaction as central characteristics, digital technologies can enable the continuous, revisited co-production of teaching-learning processes.

Wiki platforms, social networks, text and image editing, and layouts by different designers are good examples of digital spaces that can be explored as spaces relevant for assessment purposes in Physical Education. The encouragement of students to use digital affordances to engage with concepts or aspects associated with the content of classes (especially social themes and personal beliefs) are some of the elements that favour student engagement in digital learning activities.

To enable such an engagement, the teacher needs to read and listen carefully to student productions and manage and curate them. In the case of the vignette that opens this chapter, the students declared an interest in thinking about transgender athletes in sports competitions and committed to further developing the content of this topic with the teacher. Specifically on the topic of transgender athletes in sports competitions, there is still a perceived resistance to welcoming these subjects either due to the athletes' context (e.g., type of championship, age of the competitors, etc.) or the individual beliefs of the general population in embracing diverse identities (Tanimoto & Miwa, 2021). Numerous narratives emerge for and against the free participation of those athletes in competitions. With broad access to narratives on the web (e.g., social networks, journalistic portals, blogs, video platforms, and others), it is natural that students want to discuss such a powerful subject in Physical Education classes. This is an indicative example that shows how social pedagogy gains more and more meaning by articulating social themes with teaching content in Physical Education and sport. Instilling openness to thinking about new ways of experiencing sport is also a role of education. From the social pedagogy perspective, listening and acting attentively to the teaching dynamics is a formative exercise for helping students listen and act critically concerning social dynamics and influences.

Assessment as Listening, Production, and Dissemination of Knowledge: Activating Technologies

Inspired by media-education theory (Fantin, 2011), the teacher in the vignette can achieve his objective of teaching sports collaboratively by sharing responsibilities for instruction and assessment as listening, production, and socialisation of knowledge. During classes, the teacher can keep some elements common to teaching sports,[1] such as technical issues and sports tactics, in addition to the relationship between sport, mental well-being and healthy lifestyles. In alignment with media-education theory (Fantin, 2011), we argue that the following dimensions of technology can further support and challenge teachers' and students' efforts to co-construct knowledge and assessment processes within the classroom:

- **The technological dimension**. Technology can be perceived/used instrumentally, for example, as a tool to facilitate teaching. This dimension is known as 'educating *with* media and technology'.
- **The critical dimension**. Technology and media become an object of study in which students are motivated to understand and position themselves critically, interpreting the content in various ways. For example, teachers can use films to explore media influences on body stereotypes or lifestyle choices. This dimension is known as 'educating *for* media and technology'.
- **The productive and creative dimension**. Media and technology are used as a language for social interaction and communication. In this sense, the focus is on proposing that the students produce media narratives and use them to express themselves. This dimension is known as 'educating *through* media and technology'.

A possible organisation of a teaching unit can articulate traditional teaching aspects with more collaborative strategies – as those found within social media – and facilitate the collective construction of new learning syntheses through narratives created by the students (Araújo, 2017; Araújo et al., 2016; Chaves et al., 2015). As shown in Figure 10.1, six pedagogical

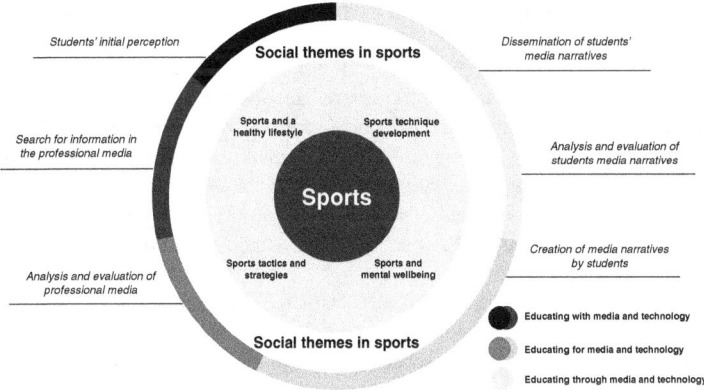

Figure 10.1 Organisation of the teaching unit (Authors' © 2023).

moments can be addressed when the organisation of the teaching unit is addressed in this way.

Based on **students' initial perception**, the teacher is invited to debate the selected transversal theme (e.g., transgender athletes in sports competitions), mediated by the speeches and narratives available in the various digital channels and communication media. This is a way of diagnosing students' reading of the world and identifying their impressions. Teachers and students can use these moments to understand that the learning process needs to consider each person's experience with their different information sources.

The **search for information in the mass media** is the space for media exploration. The teacher needs to invite students to go beyond the school space (classroom, library, sports fields) and its supporting study materials (books, notebooks, handouts, etc.) and venture into various media statements (social networks, portals news, blogs, online newspapers, influencers). Students are asked to systematise the information they find and highlight the elements that most attract their attention. The moment becomes vital for dialogue with students' social context, making the school space a recovery of everyday life and a reflection on life mediated by technology.

The **analysis and evaluation of mass media** is when students need to be equipped/prepared to read the media apparatus and understand, to some extent, the media's grammar, and the daily forms of meaning production. This reading promotes a shift in perspective to reflect on how technology changes our sensitivity and perception of sports.

In creating **media narratives by students**, we invite the teacher to promote the empowerment of the expressive space that media provides to their students. If previously the spaces for interacting with media proposed only one communication route (sender–receiver), nowadays we share the idea of network communication, in which everyone can be a *prosumer* of discourse (as highlighted in Table 10.1), almost always using platforms like those of large communication networks in their multiple modal languages.

In analysing and evaluating **students' media narratives**, it is time to debate and dialogue about the discourses created by students and how they can deconstruct forms already reified by mass media. *May the students' media narratives be considered a synthesis of learning? Is there a contrast between students' narratives and mass media narratives?* These questions can be debated and deepened in the specificities of pedagogical experiences in the most diverse contexts.

Disseminating students' media narratives is the pedagogical moment to generate and disseminate learning syntheses. All productions can be communicated/disseminated within the school community to give visibility to students' creations and expand debates. Furthermore, inviting media professionals, athletes, and community members may help to gain visibility of students' creations.

By following the proposed structure, teachers and students can work critically on the themes presented through sports and the meaning socially attributed to their content. The use of non-linear forms of communication can support new forms of elaborating sport content and narratives, besides producing learning syntheses through the media-technological language that is massively consumed.

How sports are experienced (i.e., historically focused on experiencing sports as technique) can nowadays be expanded using varying languages, expressions, impressions, and forms of learning about sport. When teachers and students express their knowledge through oral, visual, or written languages, they can debate and validate them. There are several ways to make this production reverberate nowadays, including the possibility of sharing production (process and products) on online platforms, which, due to their characteristic of building networks, can rhizomatically produce welcoming and resistance effects, always enabling new readings (see Table 10.2).

Practitioners' Voice

Seeking to think with the teacher in our vignette, we propose planning for their teaching unit, one which considers the interests of their students, the classroom spaces, and types of information that can be accessed to facilitate points of collaboration and reflection. As a principle of collective action between teachers and students, collaboration is vital to operationalising the proposal we seek to summarise in Table 10.2. Teachers can use our suggestions to reorganise their practice for a teaching experience that will renew their classroom culture.

It is essential to highlight that, unlike traditional forms of Physical Education assessment, the process proposed in this chapter is continuous and is not restricted to the product disseminated as students' media narratives (final stage).

Table 10.2 Pedagogical moments of the teaching unit

Pedagogical moments	Triggering actions	Action spaces
Students' initial perception	Debate the participation and exclusion of transgender athletes in sporting competitions.	Classroom
Search for information in professional media	Search for news, regulations, information, and decisions about the participation of transgender athletes in sporting competitions.	News portals, repositories, video sharing platforms, social networks, audio streaming services, influencers, etc.
Analysis and evaluation of professional media	Provide students with tools regarding the production of the chosen media support	Infographics, eBooks, sites, repositories, blogs, podcasts, video classes, digital magazines, apps, etc.
Creation of media narratives by students	Foster creativity, curiosity, expressiveness, pleasure, and protagonist	Diverse spaces (home, library, classroom, etc.)
Analysis and evaluation of students' media narratives	Debate and dialogue about discourses created by students	Classroom
Dissemination of students' media narratives	Share the construction process and the developed products in and out of the school	Scientific and school events, repositories, sites, video sharing platforms, social networks, audio streaming services, school fairs, etc.

Based on the principles of social pedagogy, we understand that it is possible to perceive everyone's learning as a process that has the starting point in students' initial perception (stage 1) and has deepened in the subsequent stages until the production and dissemination of the syntheses of the teaching unit.

In the high school reality in the State of Rio Grande do Norte (Brazil), this teaching sequence has already been tested, and the results of the products were exciting. We can highlight the pedagogical experience materialised at the Federal Institute of Education, Science, and Technology of Rio Grande do Norte in Parnamirim, which took place in 2019 and was published in the doctoral study of Batista (2021). The pedagogical experience of this teacher always addresses a social theme related to the teaching content (sports, dance, gymnastics, etc.), considering the students' knowledge and media research on the topic to produce learning syntheses on the chosen theme. One semester, the teacher suggested producing digital magazines to explore the teaching theme. During the classes, the teacher proposed strategies to enrich the content, such as conducting research, interviews, and writing opinion articles to strengthen the magazine's narrative and promote the construction of knowledge and the debate on the addressed social theme and its relations with Physical Education (Batista et al., 2022).

As social pedagogy believers, we suggest assessment moments are more reflective and collaborative than classification. In these terms, while social pedagogy needs more time to be recognised in educational policies, we invite all teachers to experiment with new assessment designers, as suggested in this chapter.

> **Advice from the Field**
>
> When you sit in a teaching and learning space with your student, understand that every moment is conducive to assessment. Collecting elements throughout the teaching trajectory makes the path richer in data that can be useful in completing the teaching unit. Therefore, the teacher needs to be attentive to all types of news or social facts that may link to their pedagogical practice.
>
> From another point of emphasis, the teacher needs to cross languages when dealing with any Physical Education content. Such an attitude can enrich the knowledge acquisition process. Even those experiments that are very specific, such as the use of monitoring technologies (pedometers, accelerometers, etc.), we suggest transposing the data measured on these devices to other spaces (including the non-digital ones) to understand the processes of creating them and how the interpretation of data may affect us. It is also possible to always observe forms of noteworthiness about any data or practice in Physical Education as the beginning of a teaching–learning–assessing trajectory with social relevance and pedagogical meaning.

Key Points

- Assessment as a learning-listening practice.
- Implementation of assessment practices related to diverse languages.
- Investigation of language practices of children and youth in digital culture.
- Pedagogical moments based on media-education.

Summary

Assessing is a challenging task. It requires the teacher to follow a path closer to the students and the process of building learning. In this task, we must recognise which languages (oral, written, visual) are present in our daily school

Digitally Supported Assessment in Physical Education 143

lives. We can establish that our assessment processes can criticise, use, create, or remix with these languages. In our vignette, the teacher needed to dialogue to understand what was happening in his students' conversations. Investing in a shift from 'assessment as judgment' to 'assessment as mediation to understand' – where we are in our learning and what we need to do to achieve what we want – is an exercise that will demand listening, dialogue, and experimentation in our daily school lives.

Reflection Questions and Activities

1 Has your conception of assessment aligned with a communication process between teacher and students?
2 Have the assessment instruments you use provoked movements of reflection, social issues, integration, and knowledge for your students?
3 How can technologies articulate emerging social themes with social pedagogy in assessment practices? Give us some examples.

Note

1 The teacher, in his/her social and school contexts, can activate other school physical Education teaching aspects.

References

Araújo, A.C., Batista, A.P., Sousa, D.Q.O., Barros, J.M.A., Oliveira, M.R.R., Tinôco, R.G. (2016). *Megaeventos esportivos e seus legados: reflexões sobre Copa do Mundo 2014 a partir da Mídia-Educação*. Natal, EDUFRN.
Araújo, A.C. (2017). *Um olhar estético sobre o telespetáculo esportivo: contribuições para o ensino do esporte na escola*. Natal, EDUFRN.
Batista, A.P. (2021). *Educação Física e Recursos Educacionais Digitais: uma intervenção pedagógica no Ensino Médio Integrado do Instituto Federal de Educação, Ciência e Tecnologia do Rio Grande do Norte*. [Doctoral dissertation, Universidade Federal do Rio Grande do Norte] Natal/RN, 2021. https://repositorio.ufrn.br/handle/123456789/32490
Batista, A.P., Andrade, E.R., & Melo, J.P. (2022). Produção de revistas digitais como estratégia de ensino do conteúdo esporte nas aulas de educação física no ensino médio. *Revista de Educação Física, Saúde e Esporte, 5*(1), 133–147. https://refise.ifce.edu.br/refise/article/view/158
Certeau, M. (2014). *A invenção do cotidiano: 1. Artes de fazer*. Vozes.
Chaves, P. N., Barros, J. M. A., Sousa, D. Q. de O., Costa, A. L. S., & Araújo, A. C. de. (2015). Construindo diálogos entre a mídia–educação e a Educação Física: uma experiência na escola. *Motrivivência*, 27(44), 150–163. https://doi.org/10.5007/2175-8042.2015v27n44p150

Fantin, M. (2011). Mídia-educacão: aspectos históricos e teórico-metodológicos. *Olhar de Professor*, *14*(1), 27–40. https://doi.org/10.5212/OlharProfr.v.14i1.0002.

Freire, P. (1987). *Ação Cultural para a liberdade: e outros escritos*. Paz e Terra.

Freire, P. (1998a). *Pedagogy of freedom: Ethics, democracy, and civic courage*. Rowman & Littlefield.

Freire, P. (1998b). *Teachers as cultural workers: Letters to those who dare to teach*. West-view Press.

Freire, P. (2000). *Pedagogy of the oppressed* (30th Anniversary ed.). Continuum.

García-Galera, M., & Valdivia, A. (2014). Media prosumers. Participatory culture of audiences and media responsibility. *Comunicar*, *43*, 10–13. https://doi.org/10.3916/C43-2014-a2

López-Pastor, V.M., Kirk, D., Lorente-Catalán, E., MacPhail, A., & Macdonald, D. (2013). Alternative assessment in physical education: A review of international literature. *Sport, Education and Society*, *18*(1), 57–76. https://doi.org/10.1080/13573322.2012.713860

López-Pastor, V.M., Pascual-Arias, C., & Sonlleva, C. (2022). La Evaluación Formativa y compartida en todas las etapas educativas. In C. Pascual-Arias, C., V.M López-Pastor, & M. Sonlleva (Eds.), *Buenas prácticas de Evaluación Formativa y Compartida en todas las etapas educativas* (pp. 29–27). Miño y Dávila.

Moura, A., Graça, A., MachPhail, A., & Batista, P. (2020). Aligning the principles of assessment for learning to learning in physical education: A review of literature. *Physical Education and Sport Pedagogy*, *26*(4), 388–401. https://doi.org/10.1080/17408989.2020.1834528

Tanimoto, C., & Miwa, K. (2021). Factors influencing acceptance of transgender athletes. *Sport Management Review*, *24*(3), 452–474, https://doi.org/10.1080/14413523.2021.1880771

Toffler, A. (2022). *The third wave: The classic study of tomorrow*, Random House Publishing Group.

Additional Resources

Batista, A.P., Oliveira, M.R.R. de, & Araújo, A.C. (2023). A produção de Recursos Educacionais Digitais (REDs) na Educação Física escolar. *Cadernos Do Aplicação*, *36*(1), 1–10. https://doi.org/10.22456/2595-4377.132437

Cavalcante, E., & Araújo, A.C. (2022). Digital educational resources in school physical education: an exploratory study on the MEC RED platform. *Motriz: revista de educação física*, *28*(1), e10220002222. https://doi.org/10.1590/S1980-6574202200002222

Part V
A Summary of Social Pedagogy in Physical Education

11 Insights on Social Pedagogy as Human-Centred Physical Education Practice

Aspasia Dania

This edited book aimed to initiate a practice-informed discussion on the educational qualities of enacting social pedagogy in Physical Education. With a focus on the educative relationship between teachers, students, and the broader context (e.g., classroom, school, community), the authors adopted various approaches and perspectives to propose an overarching educational paradigm for organising Physical Education as social pedagogy praxis. Within each chapter and (national) context, the way social pedagogy could enable changes in Physical Education at the curriculum, instruction, and assessment level was foregrounded, and the potential emergent adaptations in theory, policy, and practice were discussed. The authors have provided suggestions and perspectives about the potential of using social pedagogy as a holistic approach to upbringing young people through shared experiences that acknowledge them as intrinsically rich and resourceful.

The book's chapters resettle our understanding of why and how Physical Education needs to adopt an alternative perspective in the upbringing of youth in and through various movement forms and contexts. By summarising the research and practice-based perspectives presented by the authors, we are directed towards seven basic take-home messages:

- All students have unlimited learning potential, and thus, inclusion and the absolute belief that every student must succeed are essential.
- Purposefully shared activities can have therapeutic and preventive value since they enable students to develop a common interest, learn new things together and discover different aspects of themselves and others.
- Well-being, meaningfulness, and happiness facilitate holistic learning. Such learning may occur within activities that nurture curiosity and cognitive development, create joyful emotional connections, and facilitate students' embodied engagement with the learning experience.
- Social pedagogical practice is deeply rooted in teachers' inner beliefs and ethical considerations. Thus, reflection stays at the core of Physical Education practice.

- Educational processes need to interrogate (uncritically) established norms and affect more comprehensive social justice and change.
- Practitioners and professionals who adopt social pedagogy in Physical Education aim to build bridges between individuals and society. Since structural and more comprehensive social-political problems or issues are at play, a collaboration between disciplines and sectors is needed.

The multiplicity of enactments and perspectives adopted by the authors in this book strengthens our belief about the educational value of social pedagogy within school Physical Education. As shown in the different chapters, social pedagogy in Physical Education does not seek to create norms/standards to describe, understand, and explain how individuals and groups involve themselves in educational processes. Instead, it aims to create learning environments and cultures where students can ask, give, and receive help, advice, guidance, and support to improve their standard of living. It is about enabling students to become empowered and critically active citizens with the resources to sustain their well-being throughout life.

Such a paradigm shift is needed in modern Physical Education. Whether at an individual or collective level, students live in complex social and cultural contexts, with or without problems. The social and the individual are both single and continuous dimensions of their lives by which it is very difficult, if not impossible, to discern where one begins and the other ends. As such, it is more authentic and relevant for students to be the 'seekers' or 'creators' of educational rules and processes rather than their followers. For this purpose, social pedagogy attempts to change the classic '*It should be*' imperative into a probabilistic one, 'It could/maybe if' and even more into a practical or authentic one, 'What can we do together to live a better life?'

Social pedagogy can form a basis for ground educational discourse that can change Physical Education practice in the long run. Since education and policy have different temporalities (e.g., policies must respond quickly to societal problems), we expect that change within Physical Education will occur as a slower process that cannot be urged to present evidence immediately in the form of compartmentalised learning outcomes. The change would primarily mean the (re)establishment of a group ethos within Physical Education classrooms (e.g., what it means to work together as a group) and a strengthening of social cohesion to prevent marginalisation. The best way of achieving such a change is by conceptualising a social pedagogy of Physical Education as praxis. Such a framework could enable school-based Physical Education to move away from what we see as its dominant narrow technical and highly instrumental incarnation. As such, this book is novel and important as it initiates a practice-informed discussion and sets the first step in establishing multi-sectoral synergies towards this direction.

Index

Note: **Bold** page numbers refer to tables; *italic* page numbers refer to figures and page numbers followed by "n" denote endnotes.

academic: culture 55; knowledge 66; skills 66
activist teachers *see* nurturing activist teachers
adaptability 14
adaptive expertise 62
anti-oppressive practice 110
antiracism 107
Armour, K.M. 34
assessment 42, 121–132; activating technologies 138–140; athletics, worksheet **130–131**; communication process 136–138, **137**; cumulative 41; dance, worksheet **130–131**; digitally supported 134–142; 'Me in Physical Education' approach 123, **124–127**; multidimensional 43–44; plans 64–65, **65**; practitioners' voice 140–142, **141**; triadic 70, **71**
asset-based feedback **13**
autonomy-supportive approach 36

Batista, A.P. 141
belonging 45; connectedness and 17; social 40
Bildung 9, 20, 29n1
Bishop, R. 67
Borland, J. 71–72

Camiré, M. 106, 107
caring relations 16
change, as relational endeavour 24, *25*
classrooms: belonging 17; co-constructed 25; co-contributors 82, 87; connectedness 17; culture 27, 140;

ethical behaviours 22; interactions 66; oppression 81; relationships 22; traditional power relationships 80
closeness 16, 26–27
co-construction 1, 123, 138; activities 92, 93; classroom space 25; learning environment 64
co-creating inclusive learning experiences 82
collaborative games and activities 67–70; critical tension 68; goal of 69; issues **69**; subtle shift 69
collective action: boundary-crossing 53; bridge-building 53; Common Third 53; definition of 53; effectiveness of 54; empowering in-service teachers 57–58; formations 53; Physical Education workforce system 54–56; preservice Physical Education teachers 56
Common Third 10, 22, 23, *23*, 37, 53
Communication, Connection, Contribution, and Creation (4Cs) 24
communication 28; network 140; non-linear forms of 140; process, assessment 136–138, **137**
Concepts of Social Pedagogy (CSP): Common Third 10; Creativity 15; Diamond Model 14; explanations 9, **10–11**; Head-Heart-Hands 12; Participation 12; Preparing for Participation 12; three Ps (Professional, Personal, Private) 15
conformity 52

Index

confrontational learning 27
connectedness 17
consciousness: critical 111, 114–115; praxis and 81
consequentialist ethics 44
constructivism 91
cooperating teachers (CTs) 36, 42, 43
critical awareness 14, 109
critical consciousness 111, 114–115
critical thinking 65, 91, 106
cross-discipline collaboration 57
cultural humility: definition of 111; parents, progression for 113; PETE facilitators, progression for 113–114; Physical Education teachers, progression for 113
culturally responsive teaching 65–67; deficit thinking 66; example of **68**; relationships first approach 67; students' differences 67
culture: academic 55; classroom 27, 140; competence 111; learning 135; sport 40; togetherness 55
curriculum 19–28, 66; assessment 42; diversity as cultural richness 37; ethics of care 37; foundational educational objectives 41; foundational social pedagogies 42; Game Based Approaches 92; learning 42; planning 25; social pedagogy approach 41; teaching 42
cyberbullying 92

Dania, A. 16–17
Debbouze, A. 28
decision-making 17, 24, 42
deficit approach 36
deficit-based language **13**, 66
deficit/therapeutic perspective 12
deficit thinking 66
democracy 24, 78
Diamond Model 14, 21, *22*, 37
digitally supported assessment 134–142
digital platforms 58
discrimination 78, 92
disseminating students' media narratives 140
diversity 44–45, 106; as cultural richness 37; multiculturalism and 44; social justice 111
duty ethics 44

empowering in-service teachers 57–58
ethics: of care 37, 44; classroom behaviours 22; consequentialist 44; duty 44; virtue 44
extracurricular sports activities 36

Farias, C. 40, 41
feedback 63, 70; asset-based **13**; deficit **13**; multifaceted 70
femininity 112
formative assessment 135, 136
4Cs *see* Communication, Connection, Contribution, and Creation (4Cs)
Frapwell, A. 123
Freire, P. 81, 136

Game Based Approaches (GBA) 90; constructivism 91; humanistic values 92; simplified flow of *94*; social pedagogy and 91–93
Garrett, R. 66
globalisation 44, 45
Griffin, B. 128
group ethos 148
group-oriented work: boundary-setting 27; confrontational learning 27; correction and acknowledgement 28
gymnasium 20

Head-Heart-Hands 12
healthcare 47
heartfelt narratives 17
help-seeking 58
homogenisation 44
Hord, S.M. 57
human centered pedagogies 147–148
human development 10
humanised social relationships 45
human well-being 51

idea-sharing 58
(im)migration 35, 44
implementation fidelity 16
inclusive leadership 109
inequity 15, 92
instructional planning 25
interdependence 22, 44, 62
interpersonal relationships 65, 93

Justice, Equity, Diversity, and Inclusion (JEDI) 92, 93, *94;* affective 93; alignment **94**; cognitive 93; psychomotor 93; soccer lesson flow 93, **95–99**

K-12 school programmes 55

language(s) 26; barriers 45; deficit-based **13**, 66; dialogue 80; media-technological 140
Lawson, H.A. 51, 53
learning 8, 20, 135; co-create 64; confrontational 27; curriculum 42; decision-making 24; interpersonal relationships 65; negotiated 64–65, **65**; outcomes 90; pathways 13; peer-assisted 42; professional 83–84; relational 9; self-regulated 70; teaching and 22, *23*

mass media 140; analysis and evaluation of 139; search for information 139
MBA *see* model-based approaches (MBA)
meaning-making 92
media narratives, students 139–140
'Me in Physical Education' approach 123, **124–127,** 129
mental health 92, 107
mentoring process 43
Mesquita, I. 41
Middle East 44
mild-mannered suggestion 27
model-based approaches (MBA) 89–101; Game-Based Approaches 91–93; Justice, Equity, Diversity, and Inclusion 93, **94,** *94;* social pedagogy 91–93
modelling, nurturing activist teachers 84–85
motor skills 42
Moura, A. 135
movement subcultures 39
multiculturalism 44
multidisciplinary approach 33–47
multi-sectoral synergies 148
multi-systemic integrated approach 37

negotiated learning 64–65, **65**
networked improvement communities 53
networking 37, 43
Newcomer Immigrant Children (NIC) 35–37, 45; background and purpose 35–36; multidisciplinary social pedagogy approach 37, **38**; school community 36; social pedagogy educational intervention 36
Noddings, N. 16
Norley, J. 127–129

normative life skills 106
nurturing activist teachers 77–86, *79;* challenging stereotypes and assumptions 80; co-creating inclusive learning experiences 82; intention of 77; listening and trusting students 80; modelling 84–85; oppressive social injustices 81; PETE practices 81–84; positionality and privileges 83; professional learning 83–84; traditional power relations 80; transformative journey of 79–80

operationalisation 108–110
oppression 77; institutional and systemic levels 109; interrogating and de-naturalising 78; power imbalances and forces 107; social identity 108; social injustices 81

parents, progression of 113
participatory democracy practices 24
pedagogical intervention mediation 43; cyclical and responsive support 43; professional practice, multidimensional assessment of 43–44
pedagogy 1, 8; case 33–47; competence 37; conversations to enable closeness 26–27; interrelated complexity 122, *123;* as philosophy-in-use 2; social justice 78; society 14; value of sport 39–40; *see also* social pedagogy
peer-assisted learning 42
peer-caring 45
peer-mentoring activities 45
philosophical aids 44
physical activity 15, 24; opportunities 64; self-esteem 17; self-identified barriers 64
Physical Education 1–3, 20, 61–72, 104–115; assessment approaches 121–132; asset-based feedback **13**; classes 36; classroom structure 24; curriculum 19–28; deficit-based language **13**; digitally supported assessment 134–142; discrimination 78; extracurricular sports activities 36; individual emancipation 10; model-based approaches 89–101; Newcomer Immigrant Children 35–37; outcomes of 51; practice 9–16, **13**; preservice

152 Index

teachers 36; progression, teachers 113; school-based 51, 55–56; social integration 10; social pedagogy principles in 21–24; social pedagogy, rationale for 8–9; as social system 52–54; syn-epistemic wholeness of 50–59; teachers, implications 110
Physical Education Teacher Education (PETE) 37, 52, 55; facilitators 110, 113–114; mentoring process 43; nurturing activist teachers in 77–86; pedagogical intervention mediation 43–44
physical educators 3, 25, 27; implications 105; principles 110
Portugal 35, 36
positionality 83
positive reinforcement 22
poverty 10, 12
praxis 2, 81, 109; educational 8
pre-service teachers (PSTs) 78, 82
privileges 83
problem-solving 56, 93
professional learning communities (PLCs) 53, 83–84; class-level 57; collective action 57; school-based 56; The Three Ps 57–58
prospective teachers (PSTs) 42; group identity 43; legitimacy 42; professional practice 43; school community 42
prosumer concept 136, **137**
proximal networking 43
psychomotor 93

reflection 8, 26, 29, 42, 55, 71, 112, 140; phase **71**; positionality 83; privileges 83
relationality 1
relational learning 9
relationships 15, 16, 24, 109; classroom 22; first approach 67; fostering Physical Education preservice teacher growth 57; interpersonal 65; teacher-student 22, *23;* teaching and learning, mediators of 22, *23*
religious beliefs 44

sameness 52
school-based Physical Education 51, 55–56
school community 36
school shootings 92
self-critical thinking 42

self-esteem 8, 17
self-identified barriers 64
self-image 17
sense of belonging 42, 62, 67, 111
sense of possibility 8
shared assessment 135, 136
Simonsen, M. 85, 86
soccer lesson flow 93, **95–99**
social belonging 40
social capital 40
social constructs 51
social determinants 51
social development 40, 42
social education 1
social exclusion 10
social inclusion 35–37
social inequities 107
social injustice 81, 107
social integration 10
socialisation process 55
social justice 77–79, 104–115; critical consciousness 114–115; cultural competence 111–112; cultural humility 112–114; level of awareness 108; level of practice 108; level of reflexivity 109; life skills 105, *107;* normative approaches 106; operationalisation 108–110; programming continuum *107;* transformative approaches 106
social media 58, 138
social pedagogical case: background and purpose 35–36; educational intervention 36; multidisciplinary social pedagogy approach 37, **38**; Newcomer Immigrant Children 35–37; ontological view 33–34; school community 36
social pedagogy 1–3, 104–115, 121–132; caring relations 16; change as relational endeavour *25;* child in need 14; closeness 16, 26–27; curriculum and instruction 25; digitally supported assessment 134–142; foundational 42; Game Based Approaches and 91–93; group-oriented work 27–28; humanistic values 20; ideological foundation 13; insights 147–148; model-based approaches and 89–101; multidisciplinary approach 33–47; norms 14, 15; practices 7–16, 24–28; principles of 19–28; prosumer concept and relation **137**; rationale,

Physical Education 8–9; relationships 15; sport contribution to 37–40; strategies 61–72; students, educate themselves 23–24; teaching and learning, relationships 22, *23;* theory 7–16; tools **26**; transdisciplinary 14; work with children and youth 21–22, *22*
social reality 15
social service 45–47; healthcare 47; higher education 47; integrated approach 46; liaising intervention 46–47; methodology 46; school 47; social worker's positioning 45
social skills 69, 122
social solidarity 62
social system 12, 52–54
social transformations 55
social wealth 44, 45
social welfare 51
social well-being 10
social worker's positioning 45
societal membership 10
societal sectors 52
soft skills 128
Sommers, W.A. 57
sport(s): coaching 90; contribution 37–40; pedagogical value of 39–40; pluralism 39
Sport Education 22, 23
sport participation: Immigrant Children 35–37; social pedagogy approach 41
sport sociology 37; belonging 45; diversity 44–45; (im)migration 44; peer-caring 45; philosophical aids 44; time 45
status quo 78, 79
stereotypes 138; challenging 80; negative 66
strategies 1, 2, 24, 43, 61–72, 108; assessment plans 64–65, **65**; cognitive 93; collaborative games and activities 67–70, **69**; culturally responsive teaching **68**; negotiated learning 64–65, **65**; social justice 112; Student Course Committee 63, **64**; students as co-contributors 63; triadic assessment 70
Student Course Committee strategy 63, **64**

students 27, 43; affective 93; assessment approaches 41, 121–132; as co-contributors, programme and unit design 63; cognitive 93; collaborative games and activities 67–70; emotional needs 57; grading 41; individualised task 42; initial perception 139; learning 57; listening and trusting 80; media narratives 139–140; psychomotor 93; triadic assessment 70; valuable resource 67
supportive networks 13
syn-epistemic wholeness 50–59
systemic approach 66

teacher-student relationship 22, *23*
teaching: culturally responsive 65–67, **68**; curriculum 42; Game Based Approaches 92; group-oriented 27; interpersonal relationships 65; learning and 22, *23;* normative life skills 106; organisation of 138, *139;* pedagogical moments **141**; strategy 62; transformative 107; youth life skills 106
teamwork 40, 56
technologies: activating 138–140; critical dimension 138; productive and creative dimension 138; role of 136–138, **137**
three Ps 15, 57–58
traditional power relations 80
transformative teaching approach 107
transgender athletes 137
triadic assessment: discussion and feedback 70; empowerment 70; self-regulated learning 70; three-phase process of 70, **71**

Ukraine 44
UNESCO 44
unlimited learning potential 147

values-led approaches 3, 8, 16
virtue ethics 44

Whole School, Whole Community, Whole Child (WSCC) 53–54
work-role conflicts 56
World Health Organization 51
Wrench, A. 66

For Product Safety Concerns and Information please contact our EU representative GPSR@taylorandfrancis.com
Taylor & Francis Verlag GmbH, Kaufingerstraße 24, 80331 München, Germany